move up

move up

Elementary
Teacher's Book

B

MACMILLAN
HEINEMANN
English Language Teaching

Simon Greenall

Macmillan Heinemann English Language Teaching, Oxford

A division of Macmillan Publishers Limited

Companies and representatives throughout the world

ISBN 0 435 29873 9

Layout by eMC Design
Cover design by Stafford & Stafford

Note to teachers
The two tests and Practice Book Answer Key at the back of this book may be photocopied for use in class without the prior written permission of Heinemann English Language Teaching. However, please note that the copyright law, which does not normally permit multiple copying of published material, applies to the rest of this book.

Author's Acknowledgments

I am very grateful to all the people who have contributed towards the creation of this book. My thanks are due to:

- All the teachers I have had the privilege to meet on seminars in many different countries and the various people who have influenced my work.
- Paul Ruben for producing the tapes, and the actors for their voices.
- The various schools who piloted the material.
- Simon Stafford for his skilful design.
- James Hunter and Bridget Green for their careful attention to detail and their creative contribution.
- Angela Reckitt for her careful management of the project.
- Jessica Rackham for her extremely thorough and efficient editorial input.
- And last, but by no means least, Jill, Jack, and Alex.

Printed and bound in Great Britain by
The Baskerville Press Ltd, Salisbury, Wiltshire

98 99 00 01 02 10 9 8 7 6 5 4 3

Contents

Introduction

Course Organization

Move Up is a general English course which will take adult and young adult learners of English from starter level to advanced level. American English is used as the model for grammar, vocabulary, spelling, and pronunciation, but other varieties of English are included for listening and reading practice. The course components for each level are as follows:

For the student	For the teacher
Student's Book	Teacher's Book
Practice Book	Class Cassette
	Resource Pack

The Student's Book has twenty teaching lessons and four Progress Check lessons. After every five teaching lessons there is a Progress Check lesson to review the language covered in the preceding teaching lessons and to present new language work relevant to the grammar, functions, and topics covered so far. Within the teaching lessons the main grammar or language functions and the most useful vocabulary are presented in boxes that allow easy access to the principal language of the lesson. This makes the focus of the lesson clearly accessible for purposes of presentation and review. Each lesson will take between 60 and 90 minutes.

The Class Cassette contains the recorded material used in the Student's Book.

The Practice Book has twenty practice lessons corresponding to the twenty teaching lessons in the Student's Book. The Practice Book extends work done in class with the Student's Book, by providing further practice in grammar, vocabulary, reading, and writing. The activities are designed for self-access work and can be used either in the class or as self-study material. Each lesson will take between 45 and 60 minutes.

The Teacher's Book contains a presentation of the course design, methodological principles, as well as detailed teaching notes. It also includes two photocopiable tests. The teaching notes for each lesson include a step-by-step guide to teaching the lesson, a discussion of some of the difficulties the learners may encounter, and more detailed methodological issues arising from the material presented. The Practice Book Answer Key is in the Teacher's Book and may be photocopied.

The Resource Pack provides extra teaching material to practice the main language points of the teaching lessons. *Move Up* is designed to be very flexible in order to meet the very different requirements of learners. The Resource Pack contains a wide variety of communicative practice activities in the form of photocopiable worksheets with step-by-step Teacher's Notes on the back. There is at least one activity for each lesson in the Student's Book and the activities can be used to extend a core teaching lesson of 60–90 minutes from the Student's Book with an average of 30 minutes of extra material for use in the classroom. They can also be used to review specific structures, language, or vocabulary later in the course.

As well as step-by-step Teacher's Notes for each activity, the Resource Pack includes an introduction which explains how to use the worksheets and offers tips on how to get the most out of the activities.

Course Design

The course design is based on a broad and integrated multi-syllabus approach. It is broad in the sense that it covers grammar and language functions, vocabulary, reading, listening, speaking, writing, and sounds explicitly, and topics, learner training, and socio-cultural competence implicitly. It is integrated in that each strand of the course design forms the overall theme of each lesson. The lessons always include activities focusing on grammar and language functions, and vocabulary. They also include reading, listening, speaking, writing, and sounds. The inclusion of each strand of the syllabus is justified by its communicative purpose within the activity sequence. The methodological principles and approaches to each strand of course design are discussed opposite.

Methodological Principles

Here is an outline of the methodological principles for each strand of the course design.

Grammar and Language Functions

Many teachers and learners feel safe with grammar and language functions. Some learners may claim that they want or need grammar, although at the same time suggest that they don't enjoy it. Some teachers feel that their learners' knowledge of grammar is demonstrable proof of language acquisition. But this is only partly true. Mistakes of grammar are more easily tolerated than mistakes of vocabulary, as far as comprehension is concerned, and may be more acceptable than mistakes of socio-cultural competence, as far as behavior and effective communication is concerned. *Move Up* attempts to establish grammar and language functions in their pivotal position but without neglecting the other strands of the multi-syllabus design.

Vocabulary

There are two important criteria for the inclusion of words in the vocabulary boxes. Firstly, they are words which the elementary learner should acquire in order to communicate successfully in a number of social or transactional situations. Secondly, they may also be words which are generated by the reading or listening material, and are considered suitable for the elementary level. However, an overriding principle operates: there is usually an activity which allows learners to focus on and, one hopes, acquire the words which are personally relevant to them. This involves a process of personal selection or grouping of words according to personal categories. It is hard to acquire words which one doesn't need, so this approach responds to the learner's individual requirements and personal motivation. *Move Up* Elementary presents approximately 800 words in the vocabulary boxes for the learner's active attention, but each learner must decide which words to focus on. The *Wordbank* in the Practice Book encourages students to store the words they need in categories which are relevant to them.

Reading

The reading passages are at a slightly higher level than one might expect for learners at elementary level. Foreign language users who are not of near-native speaker competence are constantly confronted with difficult language, and to expose the learners to examples of real-life English in the reassuring context of the classroom is to help prepare them for the conditions of real life. There is always an activity or two which encourages the learner to respond to the passage either on a personal level or to focus on its main ideas. *Move Up* attempts to avoid a purely pedagogical approach and encourages the learner to respond to the passages in a personal and genuine way before using it for other purposes.

Listening

Listening is based on a similar approach to reading in *Move Up*. Learners are often exposed to examples of natural, authentic English in order to prepare them for real-life situations in which they will have to listen to ungraded English. But the tasks are always graded for the learners' particular level. A number of different native and non-native accents are used in the listening passages, to reflect the fact that in real life, very few speakers using English speak standard American pronunciation.

Speaking

Many opportunities are given for speaking, particularly in pairwork and groupwork. Learners are encouraged to work in pairs and groups because the number of learners in most classes does not allow the teacher to give undivided attention to each learner's English. In these circumstances, it is important for the teacher to evaluate whether fluency or accuracy is the most important criterion. On most occasions in *Move Up* Elementary, speaking practice in the *Grammar* sections is concerned with accuracy, and in the *Speaking* sections with fluency. In the latter case, it is better not to interrupt and correct the learners until after the activity is ended.

Writing

The writing activities in *Move Up* are based on guided paragraph writing with work on making notes, turning notes into sentences, and joining sentences into paragraphs with various linking devices. The activities are quite tightly controled. This is not to suggest that more creative work is not valid, but it is one of the responsibilities of a coursebook to provide a systematic grounding in the skill. More creative writing is covered in the Practice Book. Work is also done on punctuation, and most of the writing activities are based on real-life tasks, such as writing letters and cards.

Sounds

Pronunciation, stress, and intonation work tends to interrupt the communicative flow of a lesson, and there is a temptation to leave it out in the interests of maintaining the momentum of an activity sequence. In *Move Up* there is work on sounds in most lessons, usually just before the stage where the learners have to use the new structures orally in pairwork or groupwork. At this level, it seems suitable to introduce the basic system of English phonemes, most of which the learners will be able to reproduce accurately because similar phonemes exist in their own language, and activities which focus on stress in words and sentences, and on the implied meaning of certain intonation patterns, are included. The model for pronunciation is standard American English.

Topics

The main topics covered in *Move Up* Elementary include personal identification, house and home, daily life, leisure activities, travel, relations with other people, health, education, shopping, food and drink, geographical location, and the environment. On many occasions the words presented in the vocabulary box all belong to a particular word field or topic.

Learner Training

Implicit in the overall approach is the development of learner training to encourage learners to take responsibility for their own learning. Examples of this are regular opportunities to use monolingual and bilingual dictionaries, ways of organizing vocabulary according to personal categories, and inductive grammar work.

Cross-cultural Training

Much of the material and activities in *Move Up* creates the opportunity for cross-cultural training. Most learners will be using English as a medium of communication with other non-native speakers, and certainly with people of different cultures. Errors of socio-cultural competence are likely to be less easily tolerated than errors of grammar or lexical insufficiency. But it is impossible to give the learners enough specific information about a culture, because it is impossible to predict all the cultural circumstances in which they will use their newly acquired language competence. Information about *sample* cultures, such as the United States and Britain, as well as non-native English speaking ones, is given to allow the learners to compare their own culture with another. This creates opportunities for learners to reflect on their own culture in order to become more aware of the possibility of different attitudes, behavior, customs, traditions, and beliefs in other cultures. In this spirit, cross-cultural training is possible even with groups where the learners all come from the same cultural background. There are interesting and revealing differences between people from the same region or town, or even between friends and members of the same family. Exploring these will help the learners become not merely proficient at the language but competent in the overall aim of communication.

Level and Progress

One important principle behind *Move Up* is that the learners arrive at elementary level with very different language abilities and requirements. Some learners may find the early lessons very easy and will be able to move quickly on to later lessons. The way *Move Up* is structured, with individual lessons of 60-90 minutes, means that these learners can confirm that they have acquired a certain area of grammar, language function, and vocabulary, consolidate this competence with activities giving practice in the other aspects of the course design, and then move on. Others may find that their previous language competence needs to be reactivated more carefully and slowly. The core teaching lesson in the Student's Book may not provide them with enough practice material to ensure that the given grammar, language functions, and vocabulary have been firmly acquired. For these learners, extra practice may be needed and is provided in both the Practice Book (for self-study work) and the Resource Pack (for classroom work).

Interest and Motivation

Another important principle in the course design is the intrinsic interest of the materials. Interesting material motivates the learners, and motivated learners acquire the lanaguage more effectively. The topics have been carefully selected so that they are interesting to adults and young adults, with a focus on areas which would engage their general leisure-time interests. This is designed to generate what might be described as authentic motivation, the kind of motivation we have when we read a newspaper or watch a TV show. But it is obvious that we cannot motivate all learners all of the time. They may arrive at a potentially motivating lesson with little desire to learn on this particular occasion, perhaps for reasons that have nothing to do with the teacher, the course, or the material. It is therefore necessary to introduce tasks which attract what might be described as pedagogic or artificial motivation, tasks which would not usually be performed in real life, but which engage the learner in an artificial but no less effective way.

Variety of Material and Language

Despite the enormous amount of research done on language acquisition, no one has come up with a definitive description of how we acquire either our native language or a foreign language which takes account of every language learner or the teaching style of every teacher. Every learner has different interests and different requirements, and every teacher has a different style and approach to what they teach. *Move Up* attempts to adopt an approach which appeals to differing styles of learning and teaching. The pivotal role of grammar and vocabulary is reflected in the material but not at the expense of the development of the skills or pronunciation. An integrated multi-syllabus course design, designed to respond to the broad variety of learners' requirements and teachers' objectives, is at the heart of *Move Up*'s approach.

RESEARCH

Heinemann ELT is committed to continuing research into coursebook development. Many teachers contributed to the evolution of *Move Up* through piloting and reports, and we now want to continue this process of feedback by inviting users of *Move Up*— both teachers and students—to tell us about their experience of working with the course. If you or your colleagues have any comments, queries, or suggestions, please address them to the Publisher, Adult Group, Heinemann ELT, Halley Court, Jordan Hill, Oxford OX2 8EJ or contact your local Heinemann representative.

Map of the Book

Lesson	Grammar and functions	Vocabulary	Skills and sounds
11 *When in Rome, Do As the Romans Do* Customs and rules in different countries	Talking about obligation *Have to/don't have to/ should(n't)/can('t)*	New words from this lesson	**Reading:** reading for main ideas **Speaking:** talking about rules and customs in different countries **Listening:** listening for main ideas; listening for specific information **Writing:** writing advice and rules for visitors to your country
12 *Have You Ever Been to San Francisco?* Travel experiences	Present perfect (1): talking about experiences	New words from this lesson	**Reading:** reading for main ideas **Sounds:** strong and weak forms of *have* and *haven't* **Writing:** writing a postcard
13 *New York, New York!* Talking about New York	Present perfect (2): talking about unfinished events *For* and *since*	New words from this lesson	**Listening:** listening for main ideas; understanding text organisation **Speaking:** predicting; talking about experiences **Writing:** writing a paragraph about your partner
14 *Planning the Perfect Day* Favorite outings	Imperatives Infinitive of purpose	Words connected with outings	**Speaking:** talking about a perfect day **Reading:** reading for main ideas **Writing:** writing advice for planning the perfect day out
15 *She Sings Well* Schooldays	Adverbs	Adverbs and their opposites	**Sounds:** identifying attitude and mood **Reading:** reading for main ideas; reading for specific information **Listening:** listening for main ideas **Speaking:** talking about achievement at school
Progress Check Lessons 11–15	Review	Collocation	**Sounds:** words with the same vowel sound; /əʊ/ and /ɔː/; word stress and a change of meaning **Reading:** reading for specific information; focusing on unnecessary words
16 *Cruisin'!* Travel by ship and plane	Future simple (1): (*will*) for decisions	Words connected with travel by ship and plane	**Listening:** listening for specific information **Reading:** reading for specific information **Speaking:** acting out a role play in a travel agency
17 *What Will It Be Like in the Future?* Talking about the future	Future simple (2): (*will*) for predictions	Nouns and adjectives for the weather	**Listening:** listening for specific information **Reading:** predicting; reading for specific information **Speaking:** making predictions about the future
18 *Hamlet Was Written by Shakespeare* World facts	Active and passive	Verbs used for passive	**Speaking:** talking about true and false sentences **Reading:** reading and answering a quiz **Listening:** listening for specific information **Writing:** writing a quiz about your country
19 *She Said It Wasn't Far* Staying in a youth hostel	Reported speech: statements	Items connected with travel	**Reading:** reading for main ideas; reading for specific information **Listening:** listening for specific information **Writing:** writing a letter of complaint
20 *Dear Jan... Love Ruth* A short story by Nick McIver	Tense review	New words from this lesson	**Reading:** predicting; reading for main ideas **Listening:** listening for specific information **Writing:** writing a different ending to the story
Progress Check Lessons 16–20	Review	Prepositions Word association	**Sounds:** /ɔː/ and /ɔɪ/; syllable stress **Speaking:** playing *Move Up Snakes and Ladders*

1

GENERAL COMMENTS

Agatha Christie

You may like to mention that Agatha Christie created the detectives Hercule Poirot and Miss Marple, and some of her most famous books have been turned into films, such as *Murder on the Orient Express* and *Death on the Nile*.

VOCABULARY AND READING

1. Aim: to prepare for reading.

- Ask the students if they have heard of Agatha Christie. Ask them who she was, what nationality she was, what she did, when she lived, who were her famous characters.

2. Aim: to prepare for reading; to pre-teach difficult words.

- Tell the students that the article they are going to read is, in fact, not about one of Agatha Christie's characters, but about the writer herself.

- Ask the students to work in pairs. They should read the words and check that they understand them. Ask them to prepare a brief oral description of what happened to Agatha Christie.

- Ask several pairs to tell the whole class what they think happened to Agatha Christie. Of course it won't matter if they do not make an accurate description, but the process of predicting the contents of the article will be excellent preparation for reading.

3. Aim: to practice reading for main ideas.
● Ask the students to read the article and to choose the correct answer to the question in the title.

Answer
2

● Try not to explain too many words for the moment, as this will detract from the aim of the activity, which is to form a general impression of the whole passage.

4. Aim: to practice reading for specific information.
● Ask the students to look at the questions and to try and answer them from what they remember of the first reading.

● Ask the students to check their answers by reading the article again carefully.

Answers
1. False   2. False   3. False   4. True
5. False   6. False   7. True   8. False

5. Aim: to practice speaking.
● Ask the students to work in pairs and to ask and answer the questions in the Communication Activities.

GRAMMAR

1. Aim: to practice forming the past simple negative.
● Ask the students to read the information in the grammar box and then to do the activities.

● Ask the students to do this activity in writing using the negative form.

Answers
1. She didn't marry when she was fifteen. She married when she was twenty-four.
2. The police didn't find her in the car. The car was empty.
3. The police didn't say she was dead. Everyone thought she was dead.
5. Her husband didn't find her at home. He found her in a hotel 250 miles away.
6. She didn't marry a crime writer. She married an archaeologist.
8. She didn't die at the age of seventy-six. She died at the age of eighty-six.

2. Aim: to practice writing questions.
● You may like to do this activity orally with the whole class. Make sure the auxiliary *did* goes in the right place.

● Make it clear that there may be more than one possible question.

Possible Questions
1. What did Agatha Christie write?
2. When was she born?
3. Where did she live?
4. Who did she marry?
5. When did she disappear?
6. Where did her husband find her?
7. When did he find her?
8. What did Sir Max Mallowan do?

3. Aim: to practice writing questions and negatives.
● Ask the students to work in pairs and to continue to practice writing statements and negatives in the Communication Activity.

WRITING AND SPEAKING

1. Aim: to practice writing; to practice using the target structures.
● Ask students to write notes about their lives in preparation for their autobiographies.

● Ask the students to write simple sentences based on their notes.

2. Aim: to practice writing; to practice using the target structures.
● Ask the students to exchange their autobiographies and to write extra questions about their partner's autobiographies.

3. Aim: to practice writing; to practice using the target structures.
● Ask the students to re-write their autobiographies with their answers to the questions their partners asked.

● You may like to ask the students to do this last stage for homework.

2

GENERAL COMMENTS

Dates

There are a few extra details about dates which you may want to tell your students.

When you write a date you usually put a comma before the year only when the date is within a sentence.

I was born on June 20, 1981.

Although ordinal numbers (e.g. *first*) are used in dates, their abbreviated forms (*1st*) are not usually written. This will be the focus of *Vocabulary and Sounds* activity 3.

VOCABULARY AND SOUNDS

1. Aim: to present ordinal numbers.

- Write the ordinal numbers on the board and say them out loud.

- Ask the students to say the words out loud, in chorus and then individually.

- Ask the students to match the words in the box with the numbers below.

- You may like to ask students to do this activity with a partner.

2. Aim: to practice ordinal numbers.

- Ask the students to write the words for the numbers shown.

- You may want to write some extra numbers on the board.

3. Aim: to present saying and writing dates.

- Ask the students to read the information about the dates.

- ▭ Play the tape and ask the students to repeat the dates they hear.

- Continue this activity by writing a few extra dates on the board.

4. Aim: to present the months of the year; to practice saying dates.
● Ask the students to say the dates of the occasions mentioned. You may be able to add to this list.

LISTENING AND SPEAKING

1. Aim: to pre-teach some difficult vocabulary; to prepare for listening.
● Your students may not know some of these words, so it would be useful to pre-teach them before you play the tape.

● Ask the students to match the words with the special days. There may be more than one possible answer.

> **Possible Answers**
> **an important birthday:** present, letter, party, card, forget
> **passing an exam:** driver's license, certificate
> **Independence Day:** party
> **a wedding day:** present, church, reception, certificate, card, ring
> **an anniversary:** present, letter, party, card, forget

2. Aim: to practice listening for main ideas.
● Ask the students to listen and decide which special day the speaker is talking about.

● Try not to explain too much vocabulary if you want to give the students some effective practice in listening to difficult English.

● 🔊 Play the tape.

> **Answers**
> **Speaker 1:** a wedding day
> **Speaker 2:** passing an exam
> **Speaker 3:** an anniversary

3. Aim: to provide an opportunity for a second listening; to present some expressions of time.
● Ask the students to work in pairs and to try and remember as much as possible about the three passages.

● 🔊 Play the tape for students to check.

> **Answers**
> **Speaker 1:** yesterday evening, five months ago, in August
> **Speaker 2:** last Thursday, at the end of the year
> **Speaker 3:** in 1987, from nine to five, on December eleventh

GRAMMAR

1. Aim: to practice using the expressions of time.
● Ask the students to read the information in the grammar box and then to do the activities. You may need to explain or translate some of them.

● Ask the students to complete the sentences.

● Ask several students to read out their completed sentences.

2. Aim: to practice using expressions of time.
● Ask the students to work in pairs and to ask and answer the questions.

● Ask several students to tell the whole class what their answers to the questions were.

SPEAKING

1. Aim: to practice speaking; to practice using the target structures.
● Ask the students to work in pairs and write their answers to the questions on a piece of paper.

● When everyone is ready, collect the papers and give them out again to be graded. Make sure the students don't grade their own answers.

> **Answers**
> 1. 1989   6. from 214 B.C.
> 2. 1917   7. 1939
> 3. 1969   8. 1963
> 4. 1945   9. 1914
> 5. 1492

2. Aim: to practice speaking and writing; to practice using the target structures.
● Ask the students to work in two pairs and to transform the statements in their Communication Activities into questions.

> **Answers**
> **Pair A:**
> 1. When was the Kobe earthquake? (1995)
> 2. When did Martin Luther King die? (1968)
> 3. Who invented the telephone? (Alexander Graham Bell)
> 4. How old was Michelangelo when he died? (88)
> 5. Where was Joseph Stalin born? (Georgia)
>
> **Pair B:**
> 1. When was the Mexico City earthquake? (1984)
> 2. Who was the first man in space? (Yuri Gagarin)
> 3. When did the first American walk on the moon? (1969)
> 4. How many wives did King Henry VIII of England and Wales have? (6)
> 5. Where was Sigmund Freud born? (Vienna)

● Ask the students to ask and answer the questions in their groups and to keep the score.

3

GENERAL COMMENTS

Present Simple and Present Continuous

These two tenses have been presented in isolation until now, and many students whose mother tongue does not make a distinction between them may now be confusing them on a regular basis. If your students need more practice on this structure, use the extra material in the Practice Book and the Resource Pack.

American and British English

Some of your students may have learned the British English equivalents of the vocabulary in *Move Up* Elementary. If you have time, this may be a suitable lesson to explore some of the differences between American and British English. There are many differences in the vocabulary of clothes. For example:

American English	British English
underwear	(under)pants
pants	trousers
undershirt	vest
vest	waistcoat
bathrobe	dressing gown
business suit	lounge suit

VOCABULARY AND LISTENING

1. **Aim: to present the words in the vocabulary box.**
● Ask the students to show they understand the meaning of the words by pointing to items of clothing.

● If there is any confusion, ask the students to turn to the Communication Activity for an illustrated explanation of the meaning of all the words.

2. **Aim: to present the words in the vocabulary box; to present the difference between the present simple and the present continuous.**
● These vocabulary items are required for the questionnaire at the end of the lesson. This activity presents the concept question *What do you wear/are you wearing?* which allows the difference between the present simple and continuous to be illustrated.

3. **Aim: to present the words in the vocabulary box.**
● Ask the students to describe what the people in the pictures are doing. Make sure they use the present continuous, which you often use to describe a scene, because it suggests that what is happening is temporary.

4. **Aim: to practice listening; to present the difference between the present simple and continuous; to practice speaking.**
● Ask the students to listen and say who the people are. The language used on the tape identifies the four people by what they're doing and what they're wearing.

● ▭ Play the tape.

> **Answers**
> a – Erin
> b – John
> c – Louise
> d – Ed

5. **Aim: to provide an opportunity for a second listening.**
● Ask the students to fill out the chart.

● ▭ Play the tape again for students to check.

	Erin	John	Ed	Louise
What's he/she wearing?	jeans and a T-shirt	shirt and yellow tie	blue shirt, black jeans and sneakers	black dress
What's she doing?	standing by the door talking to a friend	sitting in an armchair by the window	standing by the window and laughing	standing by the television and smiling

FUNCTIONS AND GRAMMAR

1. **Aim: to focus on the uses of the present simple and continuous tenses.**

● Ask the students to read the information in the grammar and functions box and then to do the activities.

● Do this activity orally with the whole class.

Answers
1. wears
2. is smiling
3. is standing
4. is talking
5. are you working
6. stand up
7. smokes, isn't smoking
8. wears

2. **Aim: to practice describing people.**

● Ask the students to work in pairs and to describe people in the classroom.

3. **Aim: to practice using the present continuous.**

● Ask the students to write full answers to the questions about the people in the pictures.

Possible Answers
Erin is wearing jeans and a T-shirt. She's standing by the door.
John is wearing a shirt and tie. He's sitting in the armchair.
Ed is wearing sneakers, with a blue shirt and black jeans. He's laughing at something.
Louise is wearing a black dress. She's standing by the television and smiling.

READING AND SPEAKING

1. **Aim: to practice reading for main ideas.**

● The questionnaire focuses on clothes. Use it as a stimulus for discussion about what people wear and when. There will be minor differences of opinion between the students, so use this to explore attitudes about clothes. This will also have a contribution towards the syllabus of cross-cultural awareness in that if students are aware of differences within their own culture, they will be more aware of differences in other cultures.

2. **Aim: to practice speaking.**

● Ask the students to discuss their answers in pairs.

● Ask the students to discuss their answers with the whole class.

3. **Aim: to practice reading.**

● Ask the students to turn to the Communication Activity, add up their scores for the questionnaire, and read the analysis.

4

GENERAL COMMENTS

New Year's Resolution

You may need to explain that in the U.S.A., it's traditional to make a New Year's Resolution which is a firm decision on January 1 to change your life and to do things differently. It comes from a superstition that the New Year must begin happily and after a clean break with the past. It's equally traditional to break these resolutions a few days later.

You may like to ask the students if their cultures have similar traditions concerning resolutions, and if so, what the origins of those traditions are.

READING AND LISTENING

1. Aim: to practice reading for main ideas; to present examples of *going to*.
- Ask the students to read the resolutions and guess who they see in the pictures.

Answer
Dave, Andrew and Mary

2. Aim: to practice reading for main ideas; to prepare the context for *because* and *so*.
- Ask the students to match the resolutions and the reasons.

Answers
1. d 2. i 3. c 4. e 5. a 6. g 7. b 8. j 9. h 10. f

3. Aim: to practice listening for main ideas.
- Ask the students to listen to four people and to decide who is speaking. Match the number of the speaker and their name.
- ▭ Play the tape.

Answers
1. Henry and June
2. Andrew
3. Kate
4. Judy and Frank

4. Aim: to practice speaking; to provide an opportunity for a second listening.
- Ask the students to discuss what they heard in detail.
- Ask several students to tell the whole class what the speakers said.
- ▭ Play the tape again and ask the students to listen and check.

Answers
Henry and June – their jobs take up a lot of time and they're tired on the weekend.
Andrew – will take a year off before university.
Kate – always drives to work and is going to start running.
Judy and Frank – have a family and need more space.

GRAMMAR

1. Aim: to focus on the difference between the present simple and continuous of *go*.
- Ask the students to read the information in the grammar box and then to do the activities.
- You may like to do this activity with the whole class.

Answer
I go to work at nine o'clock. – something you do every day
I'm going to work at nine o'clock. – a future intention

2. Aim: to practice using *going to*.
- Ask the students to check their answers to *Reading and Listening* activity 3 in pairs.
- Now ask the students to look at the passage and say what the people are going/not going to do.
- You may like to check this orally with the whole class.

3. Aim: to practice using *going to*.
- Tell the students about your plans for the weekend. (They don't have to be true.)
- Ask the students to ask and say what they're going to do this weekend.

4. Aim: to present the use of *because*.

● Remind the students that *because* is used before the cause of something.

● Ask the students to join some of the sentences in *Reading and Listening* activity 1 and 2 with *because*.

Answers
1. Phil is going to see his friends more often **because** he stays at home all the time.
2. Andrea is going to save money **because** she spends too much.
3. Pete is going to change his job **because** he hates his work.
4. Andrew and Mary are going to travel around Europe **because** their grandparents came from there.
5. Jill and Steve are going to take Spanish lessons **because** they don't speak any foreign languages.
6. Jenny is going to spend more time with her parents **because** she never sees her family.
7. Henry and June are going to invite more friends for dinner **because** they don't entertain very much.
8. Kate is going to get in shape **because** she doesn't do enough exercise.
9. Dave is not going to take work home **because** he wants to spend more time with his children.
10. Judy and Frank are going to move **because** their house is too small.

5. Aim: to present the use of *so*.

● Remind the students that *so* is used before the consequence of something.

● Ask the students to join some of the sentences in *Reading and Listening* activities 1 and 2 with *so*.

Answers
1. Phil stays at home all the time, **so** he's going to see his friends more often.
2. Andrea spends too much, **so** she's going to save money.
3. Pete hates his work, **so** he's going to change his job.
4. Andrew and Mary's grandparents came from Europe, **so** they're going to travel around Europe.
5. Jill and Steve don't speak any foreign languages, **so** they're going to take Spanish lessons.
6. Jenny never sees her family, **so** she's going to spend more time with her parents.
7. Henry and June don't entertain very much, **so** they're going to invite more friends for dinner.
8. Kate doesn't do enough exercise, **so** she's going to get in shape.
9. Dave wants to spend more time with his children, **so** he is not going to take work home.
10. Judy and Frank's house is too small, **so** they're going to move.

VOCABULARY AND WRITING

1. Aim: to present the words in the vocabulary box.

● Check the students understand what the words mean.

● Do this collocation work with the whole class.

Answers
save money
take work home, take (Spanish) lessons
spend time
get in shape
invite friends
change my job

● Ask the students to describe what they are going to do on the weekend using the verbs in the box.

2. Aim: to practice using *going to*.

● Ask five or six students what they're going to do before they finish *Move Up* Elementary.

● Ask the students to think of two or three things they're going to do and write sentences.

3. Aim: to practice writing.

● Ask the students to think about why they are going to do the things they mentioned in 2 and write sentences.

4. Aim: to practice writing; to practice using *because*.

● Ask the students to join the sentences they have written with *because*.

● You may like to make a class collection of resolutions and put some of them on the wall to remind people of their plans. When you finish *Move Up* Elementary, read them out and find out if anyone has kept their resolutions.

5

GENERAL COMMENTS

Varieties of English

If your students found the American/British English differences in Lesson 3 interesting, here are some more differences to do with food.

American English	British English
eggplant	aubergine
cookie	biscuit
French fries	chips
chips	crisps
candy	chocolate/sweets
zucchini	courgette
bell pepper	green pepper

Cross-cultural Awareness

The information about eating out in the U.S.A. is provided not necessarily because the students should know about restaurants here, but because it allows them to reflect on eating habits and customs in their own cultures.

VOCABULARY AND LISTENING

1. **Aim: to present the words in the vocabulary box.**
- Most of these words are likely to be used in different kinds of fast food restaurants. Ask your students if they prefer fast food or more traditional restaurants.

- Ask the students which items of food and drink they can see on the menu.

> **Answers**
> cheeseburger, French fries, ice cream, pizza, salad, soda

2. **Aim: to practice using the words in the vocabulary box.**
- Ask the students to choose the word that doesn't belong.

> **Answer**
> 1. cheeseburger
> 2. spaghetti
> 3. strawberry
> 4. Jello

- Ask the students to make up their own game and to write the words on pieces of paper. When they're ready, they should swap their papers with another student, who should then find the word that doesn't belong.

- You may like to ask the students which items of food and drink they like.

3. **Aim: to prepare for listening.**
- This is a typical conversation between a cashier and a customer in a fast food restaurant. Ask the students to read the conversation and decide where the sentences should go.

> **Answers**
> 1. b   2. a   3. e   4. c   5. d   6. f

4. **Aim: to practice listening for specific information.**
- ▭ Play the conversation. Ask the students to listen and check their answers to 3.

FUNCTIONS

1. Aim: to focus on the difference between *like* and *would like*.

- Ask the students to read the information in the functions box and then to do the activities.

- You can do this activity orally with the whole class.

2. Aim: to practice speaking.

- Ask the students to act out the conversation in pairs.

- When they're ready, ask three or four pairs to act out the conversation in front of the class.

3. Aim: to practice the language for talking about prices.

- Ask the students how much some of the things on the menu cost in their country. This will provide the model the students will need for this activity.

- Ask the students to work in pairs and to ask and say how much things cost on the menu.

SOUNDS

Aim: to focus on the pronunciation of *like* and *would like*.

- 📼 Play the tape and ask the students to listen to the sentences and to check the ones they hear.

Answers
1. b   2. a   3. b   4. a   5. a   6. a

- Ask the students to read the sentences out loud.

READING AND SPEAKING

1. Aim: to pre-teach difficult vocabulary.

- Make sure the students know the meaning of the underlined words.

2. Aim: to practice reading for specific ideas.

- Ask the students to read the passage to find out what it says about the points mentioned.

Answers

types of restaurants: fast food, coffee shop, diner, family restaurant, top class restaurant

where to sit: coffee shop - you sit at the counter or at a table; family restaurant - a waiter shows you where to sit; top class restaurant - a waiter shows you where to sit

who to pay: fast food restaurant - you pay the person who serves you; coffee shop - you pay the cashier; top class restaurant - you pay the waiter

how much to tip: fast food restaurant - no need to tip; family restaurant - add 15 per cent to the check; top class restaurant - add 15 per cent to the check

other advice: fast food restaurant - put the empty container and paper in the trash can; coffee shop - you don't wait for the waitress to show you where to sit; family restaurant - you don't need to tell the waiter your name, if you don't eat everything, the waiter will bring a doggy bag; top class restaurant - you can only refuse the wine you taste if it is bad.

3. Aim: to check answers to 2; to practice speaking; to practice cross-cultural comparison.

- Ask the students to work in pairs to check their answers.

- Lead a discussion with the whole class about eating out in the United States and the students' countries.

Progress Check 1–5

GENERAL COMMENTS

You can work through this Progress Check in the order shown, or concentrate on areas which have caused difficulty in Lessons 1 to 5. You can also let the students choose the activities they would like or feel the need to do.

VOCABULARY

1. **Aim: to present some techniques for dealing with unfamiliar words.**

● Ask the students to read the advice on dealing with unfamiliar words. Explain to them (again, if necessary) that they have to develop these techniques because they won't always have a dictionary or a teacher nearby to explain everything they don't understand. Furthermore, if they do look up every word, their reading speed is greatly reduced.

● This activity is designed to show the students that they don't always have to know what a word means to understand the general sense of the passage. In this case, they aren't even able to see the whole passage.

Answers
menu, counter, empty, trash can, waitress, cashier, booths

2. **Aim: to review words for food, drink and clothes.**

● Ask the students to do this on their own, and then ask them to check their answers.

Answers
Food and drink: hamburger, cheesecake, salad, chocolate, apple
Clothes: shoes, dress, jeans, sock, shirt

● Find out how many students found all ten words.

3. **Aim: to review vocabulary from Lessons 1 to 5.**

● Ask the students to make their own word puzzles.

● When they're ready, ask the students to do each other's word puzzles.

GRAMMAR

1. **Aim: to review expressions of time.**

Answers
1. He started work **yesterday** morning.
2. We went camping **last** summer.
3. I started studying French **last** year.
4. He called me five minutes **ago**.
5. It was open **from** nine **to** five.
6. He left **at** the end of the week.

2. Aim: to review the difference in meaning between the present simple and continuous.

> **Answers**
> 1. wear 2. is standing 3. smokes
> 4. shake 5. is smiling 6. speak

3. Aim: to review the use of *going to*.
● Ask the students to write five plans or intentions using *going to*.

4. Aim: to review the use of *because*.

> **Answers**
> 1. I'd like something to eat **because** I'm hungry.
> 2. Would you like spaghetti **because** we don't have any pizza?
> 3. I'm going to see Tom Cruise's new film **because** I like him.
> 4. I'm going to live in New York **because** I like the people there.
> 5. He can't see **because** he doesn't have his glasses.
> 6. We're not going away this year **because** we went on vacation last year.

5. Aim: to review the use of *so*.

> **Answers**
> 1. I'm hungry **so** I'd like something to eat.
> 2. We don't have any pizza **so** would you like spaghetti?
> 3. I like Tom Cruise **so** I'm going to see his new film.
> 4. I like the people in New York **so** I'm going to live there.
> 5. He doesn't have his glasses **so** he can't see.
> 6. We went on vacation last year **so** we're not going away this year.

SOUNDS

1. Aim: to focus on homophones.
● ▭ Play the tape. Explain that words which sound the same but have a different spelling are called homophones.

> **Answers**
> meet – meat, their – there, know – no, sea – see, son – sun, write – right, eye – I, for – four, knows – nose, too – two

2. Aim: to focus on /uː/ and /ʊ/ .
● Ask the students to say the words out loud.

● Ask the students to put the words in two columns.

● ▭ Play the tape for the students to check. Ask them to repeat the words out loud.

> **Answers**
> /uː/: food, shoe, you, soup, do, cool, juice, boot
> /ʊ/: good, cook, book, foot, put

3. Aim: to focus on stressed syllables in words.
● Ask the students to underline the stressed syllables in the words.

> **Answers**
> banana, cabbage, potato, bacon, casual, sneakers, cashier, cheesecake, salad, hamburger, toothpaste

● ▭ Play the tape. Ask the students to check their answers and say the words out loud as they hear them.

4. Aim: to focus on polite intonation.
● ▭ Play the tape and ask the students to listen and say which speaker sounds polite.

> **Answers**
> **Polite:**
> 1. Can I help you?
> 2. Would you like a drink?

WRITING AND SPEAKING

1. Aim: to practice using the past simple; to practice writing.
● Ask the students to write questions about well-known people, places, or historical facts.

● You may like to ask them to do this for homework.

2. Aim: to practice speaking.
● Ask the students to do their quizzes in groups of four.

● Find out which group gets the highest score.

6

GENERAL COMMENTS

Customer Service Relationships

You may like to share with your students that in the United States, the relationship between customers and store clerks is friendly and polite, and dealings are often conducted on a basis of equality rather than servility or indifference. All the verbal exchanges contain the usual, sometimes elaborate, politeness formulae, and avoid abruptness and direct instructions.

When you enter a store which has clerks (unlike supermarkets), you will very often be greeted with *May I help you?* If you think the clerk can help you, then say so, but do not feel obliged to buy anything. If you prefer not to have help, you can say *It's all right, I'm just looking.* At this point, the clerk will leave you alone. In most stores you are usually welcome to pick up goods and examine them before you buy them and without asking for permission, as long as they are within reach. Goods behind the counter are there in order to be protected against theft or damage.

Find out if the students think customer service relationships are similar in their country.

SPEAKING AND LISTENING

1. Aim: to practice speaking; to present reflexive pronouns.

● These exchanges can generate a certain amount of discussion work in the process of matching the two parts, and can act as a stimulus for an improvised conversation.

● You may like to do this activity with each part of the conversation written on a separate piece of paper. Students should learn their part and go around the class saying it until they have found a suitable partner.

Answers
1. d   2. c   3. a   4. b

● Correct this activity with the whole class.

2. Aim: to practice speaking.

● Ask the students to extend their conversations with two or three sentences before and after their exchange.

● When they are ready, ask the students to act out their conversations in front of the class.

● You may like to ask your students to do this activity for homework.

3. Aim: to prepare for listening.

● Ask the students to read the conversation and to decide if the customer is buying something for herself or for someone else.

Answer
For herself

● You may like to answer a few questions about difficult vocabulary.

4. Aim: to practice listening for specific information; to present the language of saying what you'd like, making decisions and giving opinions.

● 🔊 Play the tape and ask the students to underline anything which is different from what they hear.

Answers

CLERK	May I help you?
CUSTOMER	Yes, I'm looking for a <u>sweater</u>.
CLERK	We have some <u>sweaters</u> over here. What color are you looking for?
CUSTOMER	This <u>blue</u> one is nice.
CLERK	Yes, it is. Is it for you?
CUSTOMER	Yes, <u>it is</u>. Can I try it on?
CLERK	Yes, go ahead.
CUSTOMER	No, it's too <u>small</u>. It doesn't fit me. Do you have one in a <u>bigger</u> size?
CLERK	No, I'm afraid not. What about the <u>red</u> one?
CUSTOMER	No, I don't like the color. <u>Red</u> doesn't look good on me. OK, I'll leave it. Thank you.
CLERK	Goodbye.

5. Aim: to focus on the target language; to practice speaking.

● Ask the students to correct the conversation so it follows what they heard. You may need to play the tape again.

GRAMMAR AND FUNCTIONS

1. **Aim: to focus on reflexive pronouns.**

● Ask the students to read the information in the grammar and functions box and then to do the activities.

● Ask the students if their language has reflexive pronouns or has some other way of expressing the same idea.

● Ask the students to complete the sentences.

> **Answers**
> 1. myself   2. ourselves   3. herself
> 4. yourself   5. themselves   6. himself

2. **Aim: to practice speaking; to practice using the target language.**

● Ask the students to act out the conversation in *Speaking and Listening* activity 3.

VOCABULARY AND SPEAKING

1. **Aim: to present the words in the vocabulary box.**

● Ask the students to work in pairs and to decide which items they can see in the pictures.

● Check the answers with the whole class.

> **Answers**
> chocolate, flowers, perfume, cakes

2. **Aim: to present to words in the vocabulary box.**

● Ask the students to match the different types of "containers" with the items in 1.

> **Answers**
> a box of chocolate, a package of cookies,
> a bottle of perfume, a bunch of flowers,
> a pair of jeans, a bar of soap

3. **Aim: to practice speaking.**

● Ask the students to talk about which items they buy for themselves and which they buy as gifts for other people.

4. **Aim: to practice speaking.**

● Ask the students to act out a conversation based on items in the pictures. They should use the vocabulary in 1 and 2 to help them.

● When they are ready, ask the students in turn to perform their conversations to the rest of the class.

SPEAKING

1. **Aim: to practice speaking.**

● Ask the students to work in groups and to discuss their answers to the questions.

2. **Aim: to practice speaking.**

● Ask the students to visit other groups and to find out their views on shopping.

3. **Aim: to practice speaking.**

● Ask the students to report back to their group and tell them what they've learned.

● You may like to ask each group in turn to give feedback on their discussion to the whole class.

7

GENERAL COMMENTS

Expressions with *Made*

You use *made of* to describe the material used to make something. *It's made of leather.* You use *made out of* to focus on the process of manufacture. *The child's doll was made out of sticks, wool, cloth, and cotton wool.* When the material completely changes in the process of making something, you use *made from*. *Beer is made from hops, barley, and water.* It's probably better to focus on *made of*, and to treat it as a prepositional phrase rather than a present simple passive (see Lesson 9).

VOCABULARY AND SPEAKING

1. Aim: to present the words in the vocabulary box.
- Draw shapes on the board and ask students to label them with words from the box.

- Ask the students to complete the sentences with words from the box.

Answers		
d. It's round	e. It's rectangular	f. It's light
g. It's large	h. It's small	i. It's heavy

2. Aim: to present the words in the vocabulary box.
- Ask the students to say what the things in the drawings are made of.

- Go around the classroom pointing at objects and asking *What's it made of?* Elicit a suitable response.

3. Aim: to practice using the new vocabulary.
- Ask the students to work in pairs. Student A should choose an object in the classroom, but not say what it is. Student B should ask questions, trying to guess what object Student A is thinking of.

4. Aim: to present possessive pronouns.
- Ask the students to match the conversations and the pictures.

GRAMMAR AND FUNCTIONS

1. **Aim: to focus on the formation of possessive pronouns.**

● Ask the students to read the information in the grammar and functions box, and then to do the activities.

● Ask the students to say the possessive pronouns out loud.

● Ask the students to decide which letter is often added to the possessive adjective to form the possessive pronoun.

> **Answer**
> The letter is *s*. The exception is *mine*.

2. **Aim: to focus on the difference between the possessive adjective and possessive pronoun.**

● Ask the students to choose the correct word. You may like to do this orally with the whole class.

> **Answers**
> 1. mine   2. my   3. her, mine
> 4. Who's   5. their, ours 6. Whose

3. **Aim: to practice using the language for describing objects.**

● You may like to play a round of this game with two or three students in front of the class.

● Ask students to carry on playing this game in pairs.

LISTENING AND SPEAKING

1. **Aim: to prepare for listening.**

● You may like to explain that a Lost and Found office is the place where people might find possessions which they've lost.

● Ask the students to match the numbers and the questions.

> **Answers**
> 1. e   2. f   3. h   4. a   5. d   6. i   7. b   8. g   9. c

2. **Aim: to practice listening for specific information.**

● ▭ Play the tape and ask the students to underline anything which is different from what they hear.

> **Answers**
>
> | Lost Property | |
> | --- | --- |
> | 1. Name | Ms. Jill Fairfield |
> | 2. Address | 11510 North Nevada, Springdale, Washington 92704 |
> | 3. Telephone | (509) 555-6473 |
> | 4. Lost article | a bag |
> | 5. Date of loss | July 21 |
> | 6. Time of loss | about 11 in the morning |
> | 7. Place of loss | Disneyland |
> | 8. Description | large, square, made of black nylon |
> | 9. Contents | a purse, a calculator, an address book a comb, and a newspaper |

3. **Aim: to practice speaking.**

● Ask the students to correct the information.

● ▭ Play the tape again and let the students check their answers.

4. **Aim: to practice speaking.**

● Ask the students to act out the conversation in pairs.

● Ask one or two pairs of students to act out the conversation in front of the whole class.

8

GENERAL COMMENTS

Medical Treatment

The text in this lesson gives the students an opportunity to reflect on medical treatment in the United States and in their own country. Even if they never visit the United States, or if they do, never need medical treatment, focusing on similarities and differences creates a chance to see how other cultures view illness and their relationship with the doctor.

Medical treatment in the United States is very good, but it is also very expensive, and it is essential for anyone who plans to visit or stay in the United States to have good medical insurance.

Should

Should, like *can* (Book A, Lesson 13 and Book B, Lesson 11) is a modal verb. In later levels of *Move Up*, more emphasis is given to the particular properties of modal verbs, but at this level, they are treated cursorily. In the *Grammar Review* there is a more complete description of modal verbs, but you may want to leave detailed treatment until the Pre-intermediate level.

VOCABULARY AND LISTENING

1. Aim: to present the words and expressions in the vocabulary box.

● If they have them, ask the students to use their dictionaries to do this activity.

● To keep eye contact with the students, you may like to write the four categories on the board, and ask the students to come up, in turn, and write the words under a suitable heading.

> **Answers**
> **two types of medicine:** aspirin, cough medicine
> **six medical problems or illnesses:** cold, cough, headache, sore throat, stomachache, temperature
> **four adjectives to describe how you feel:** dizzy, faint, sick, tired
> **seven parts of the body:** arm, back, finger, foot, hand, leg, toe

2. Aim: to practice listening for specific information.

● 🔲 Play the tape and ask the students to say what's wrong with each person.

> **Answers**
> **Conversation 1:** headache, cough, feels tired
> **Conversation 2:** feels sick, stomachache, headache, temperature
> **Conversation 3:** leg hurts

3. Aim: to present *should*.

● Explain that *should* is used to give advice. Write on the board the answers to activity 2, and ask students to say what each person should do.

FUNCTIONS AND GRAMMAR

1. Aim: to focus on the language of asking and saying how you feel.

● Ask the students to read the information in the functions and grammar box and then to do the activities.

● You may like to write the language in the vocabulary box under *nouns* and *adjectives*.

● Ask the students to work out the answers to the questions by looking at the examples in the vocabulary box.

> **Answers**
> 1. adjective   2. noun   3. a part of the body

2. Aim: to practice using *should*.

● Ask the students to give their advice about the people in the conversations.

3. Aim: to practice speaking; to practice using the language of asking and saying how people are.

● Ask the students to turn to the Communication Activity and act out short conversations. They can use the phrases in *Vocabulary and Listening* 3 to help them.

● When the students are ready, ask them to act out one or two of their conversations in front of the whole class.

READING AND WRITING

1. **Aim: to prepare for reading.**
- Ask the students to work in pairs and to talk about their answers to the questions.

- You may like to discuss the students' answers with the whole class.

2. **Aim: to read for specific information.**
- Ask the students to read the passage and to answer the questions in 1.

Answers
1. To the local doctor.
2. Yes.
3. At a drugstore.
4. No.
5. It doesn't say.
6. You call 911 for an ambulance.
7. Yes.
8. Yes. Most people have medical insurance to pay for treatment.

3. **Aim: to practice speaking; to prepare for writing.**
- Ask the students to compare medical treatment in the United States and in their countries.

4. **Aim: to practice writing.**
- Ask the students to prepare an advice leaflet for foreign visitors. Suggest that they use the questions in 1 to help them.

- Ask the students to write a first draft. They should then read out some of their sentences or notes to the whole class. Other students may be able to make suggestions for extra information to be included.

- Ask the students to make a second draft of the written work.

- You may like to ask students to do the last stages of this activity for homework.

9

GENERAL COMMENTS

Comparative and Superlative Forms of Short Adjectives

The adjectives presented in the vocabulary box have been selected on two criteria: they have opposites, and they have endings which illustrate the most common forms of the comparative and superlative. Together, they lend themselves to describing countries more than anything else. So, as in many lessons in the *Move Up* series, the topic of this lesson, countries and their statistics, is greatly influenced by the structures which need to be taught.

VOCABULARY AND SOUNDS

1. Aim: to present the adjectives and their opposites.

● Check that the students understand the meaning of the adjectives.

● Ask the students to match the adjectives and their opposites.

Answers
big – small, cold – hot, dry – wet,
fast – slow, high – low, old – young

2. Aim: to present the words in the vocabulary box.

● Ask the students to match the measurements and the categories.

Answers
area: square mile
length: inch, foot, yard, mile
temperature: Fahrenheit

3. Aim: to focus on stressed syllables in words.

● 💻 Play the tape and ask the students to underline the stressed syllables.

● Ask the students to listen and repeat the words.

Answers
area, average, temperature, rainfall, population, education

4. Aim: to focus on abbreviations.

● Ask the students to match the words and the abbreviations.

Answers
in. – inch
ft. – foot
yd. – yard
°F – degrees Fahrenheit
sq. mi. – square mile
mi. – mile

READING AND LISTENING

1. Aim: to practice reading for specific information.

● Ask the students to read the factfile and to decide whether the statements are true (T) or false (F) or whether no information (NI) is given.

● Check this activity with the whole class. Remember that they do not yet have to use comparatives and superlatives.

Answers
1. False 2. False 3. False 4. False
5. True 6. False 7. False

2. Aim: to practice listening for specific information.

● Ask the students to listen to Karl and to put the letter corresponding to the correct answer in the Country Factfile chart on page 20.

● 🔲 Play the tape.

Answers
1. a 2. a 3. a 4. a 5. b 6. b

3. Aim: to practice listening for specific information.

● Ask the students what else Karl mentions.

● 🔲 Play the tape and ask the students to check their answers.

Answers
Sweden is about the size of California.
January is the coldest month, July the hottest.
It rains less in Stockholm than the national average.
Some students go on to university.

GRAMMAR AND FUNCTIONS

1. Aim: to focus on the formation of comparative and superlative endings.

● Ask the students to read the information in the box and then to do the activities.

● Ask the students to do this orally with the whole class.

Answers
With -e you add -st.
With -y you drop the -y and add -ier, -iest.
With vowel + -g and -t you double the final consonant and add -er, -est.

2. Aim: to practice forming comparative and superlative forms of adjectives.

● Ask the students to use the rules in 1 to make comparative and superlative forms.

Answers
large, larger, largest
fine, finer, finest
close, closer, closest
wide, wider, widest
dirty, dirtier, dirtiest
dry, drier, driest
healthy, healthier, healthiest
heavy, heavier, heaviest
noisy, noisier, noisiest
big, bigger, biggest
hot, hotter, hottest
wet, wetter, wettest

3. Aim: to practice using comparatives and superlatives.

● Do this activity orally with the whole class.

Answers
1. The United States is bigger than Brazil.
2. It's hotter in Brazil than in the United States.
3. It's wetter in Brazil than in the United States.
4. The population in the United States is bigger than in Brazil.
6. Brazilian children are older when they start school than American children.
7. Brazilian children are younger when they can leave school than American children.

4. Aim: to practice using comparatives and superlatives.

● Ask the students to do this activity in writing on their own, and then to check their answers in pairs.

Answers
1. Sweden is smaller than Brazil.
2. Brazil is hotter than Sweden.
3. The United States is drier than Brazil.
4. The United States has the biggest armed services of the three countries.
5. The children in the United States are younger when they start school than the children in Sweden.
6. Sweden is the coldest of the three countries.

WRITING

Aim: to practice writing.

● Ask the students to choose one of the tasks in this activity. If they choose to write a factfile, you may like to ask them to do this for homework, using reference books.

● If they choose to write a paragraph, ask them to do a first draft, which they check with you, and then a second, more developed draft. They may like to do this for homework.

10

GENERAL COMMENTS

Sports

Many students like sports, and teachers may appreciate the opportunity for the students to talk about something they really enjoy.

However, it's difficult to treat the topic of sports well in a textbook, because it is relatively ephemeral and by the time the material is used in an English class, it might be out of date. This lesson simply presents the words for various sports and creates a neutral context for a popular topic to be discussed.

VOCABULARY AND LISTENING

1. Aim: to present the words in the vocabulary box.

● There are many words for sports which are the same in English as in other languages. Which words do the students recognize?

● Ask the students to decide which sports are shown in the pictures.

● If there is any confusion, ask the students to turn to the Communication Activity for an illustrated explanation of the other sports.

> **Answers**
> windsurfing, cycling, basketball, climbing

2. Aim: to check the comprehension of the new words.

● Ask the students to do this activity on their own and then in pairs.

> **Answers**
> **team sports:** football, auto racing, basketball, soccer, baseball
> **individual sports:** swimming, golf, horseback riding, climbing, windsurfing, skiing, hang gliding, cycling

● You may find students disagree as to whether auto racing is a team or an individual sport.

3. Aim: to present the new words in the vocabulary box.

● This activity involves the students' personal opinions, so make sure there is plenty of discussion at the feedback stage.

4. Aim: to practice using the new vocabulary; to prepare for listening.

● This activity can be done as discussion in small groups or with the whole class.

● You may like to ask students to raise their hands if they agree with each statement, and then count the number of "votes."

5. Aim: to practice listening for main ideas.

● 🔲 Play the tape and ask the students to check the statements the speakers agree with.

> **Answers**
>
> | | Katy | Andy |
> |---|---|---|
> | The most popular sport is baseball. | ✓ | ✓ |
> | Horseback riding is more expensive than cycling. | ✓ | ✓ |
> | Swimming is the most tiring sport. | ✗ | ✓ |
> | Hang gliding is more dangerous than windsurfing. | ✓ | ✗ |
> | Climbing is more difficult than skiing. | ✗ | ✓ |
> | Auto racing is the most exciting sport. | ✓ | ✗ |

6. Aim: to practice speaking; to provide a second opportunity for listening.

● 🔲 Ask the students to discuss their answers and then play the tape again.

GRAMMAR AND FUNCTIONS

1. Aim: to practice forming the comparative and superlative forms of adjectives.

● Ask the students to read the information in the grammar and functions box, and then to do the activities.

● Ask the students to do this activity orally in pairs.

● Correct the answers with the whole class.

> **Answers**
> 1. Horseback riding is very expensive.
>   Yes, it's **the most expensive** sport I can think of.
> 2. Auto racing is very dangerous.
>   Yes, it's **more dangerous** than skiiing.
> 3. Football is very popular.
>   Yes, it's **more popular** than golf.
> 4. Windsurfing is very difficult.
>   Yes, it's one of **the most difficult** sports I can think of.
> 5. Swimming is very tiring.
>   Yes, it's **the most tiring** sport in the world.

2. Aim: to focus on the formation of comparative and superlative forms of adjectives.

● Ask the students to choose the correct sentence.

> **Answers**
> 1. a – correct form of superlative.
> 2. a – only a superlative makes sense.
> 3. a – *best* is the superlative form.

3. Aim: to practice speaking.

● Ask the students to work in pairs and to report back on *Vocabulary and Listening* activity 4.

● You may like to ask a few students to tell the whole class what their answers were.

4. Aim: to practice forming comparatives and superlatives.

● Ask the students to make sentences using comparative and superlative forms of the adjectives which come from elsewhere in the book.

SPEAKING

1. Aim: to extend the vocabulary field; to practice speaking.

● Do this activity with the whole class. Write a list of olympic sports on the board.

2. Aim: to practice speaking.

● Ask the students to work in groups of two or three and to make a list of what they like or dislike about the Olympic Games.

● Lead a discussion with the whole class about the Olympic Games. How many people enjoy them? How many people dislike them? What do they enjoy?

Progress Check 6–10

GENERAL COMMENTS

You can work through this Progress Check in the order shown, or concentrate on areas which have caused difficulty in Lessons 6 to 10. You can also let the students choose the activities they would like or feel the need to do.

VOCABULARY

1. Aim: to present adjectives and their opposites.
- Explain that many adjectives have an opposite, and that it's useful to note it down at the same time as they note down the new word.

- Ask the students to write the opposites of the adjectives shown.

Answers
heavy – light, large – small, long – short, round– square

2. Aim: to review new words from Lessons 6 to 10.
- Ask the students to play this game in groups of three or four. You can allow up to ten minutes for it.

GRAMMAR

1. Aim: to review possessive pronouns and adjectives.

Answers
1. my, mine 2. hers 3. your
4. theirs, yours 5. my 6. my, yours

2. Aim: to review the comparative and superlative forms of adjectives.

Answers

Adjective	Comparative	Superlative
large	larger	largest
good	better	best
popular	more popular	most popular
big	bigger	biggest
comfortable	more comfortable	most comfortable
healthy	healthier	healthiest
safe	safer	safest
wet	wetter	wettest
expensive	more expensive	most expensive
tiring	more tiring	most tiring
heavy	heavier	heaviest
high	higher	highest
difficult	more difficult	most difficult

3. Aim: to review comparative forms of adjectives.

Answers
1. smaller
2. more dangerous
3. more expensive
4. colder
5. more popular
6. more exciting

4. Aim: to review the distinction between the comparative and superlative forms of adjectives.

Answers
1. largest
2. most expensive
3. smaller
4. more tiring
5. most popular

5. **Aim: to review the language of saying how you feel.**

> **Possible Answers**
> 1. dizzy, sick, tired
> 2. leg, arm, back
> 3. a temperature, a headache, a stomachache

6. **Aim: to review the language for giving advice.**

● Ask the students to think of suitable advice to give.

SOUNDS

1. **Aim: to focus on words which rhyme.**

● The spelling of these words does not give much of a clue to their pronunciation. Say the words out loud and ask the students to group them according to those which rhyme.

● 🔊 Play the tape and ask the students to check, and to repeat each word as they hear it.

> **Answers**
> could, wood, good; half, laugh; said, head, red

2. **Aim: to focus on /eɪ/ and /aɪ/.**

● Ask the students to say the words out loud and to put them in two columns.

> **Answers**
> /eɪ/: face, May, eight, maid, tray
> /aɪ/: fine, sign, night, lie

● 🔊 Play the tape and ask the students to check their answers. Ask them to say the words out loud at the same time.

3. **Aim: to focus on stress patterns in words.**

● Ask the students to match the words and the stress patterns.

> **Answers**
> reception, receiver, umbrella
> windsurfing, temperature
> rectangular

● 🔊 Play the tape and ask the students to listen and check their answers. As they listen, they should repeat the words.

4. **Aim: to focus on word stress in sentences.**

● Remind the students that the speakers are likely to stress the words which they consider to be important.

> **Answers**
> Customer   And I must have lost it then.
> Official   Just say your name again, ma'am.
> Customer   Mary Walter.
> Official   May I have your address and phone number?
> Customer   East 23010 'E' Street, Toronto, 758-8956.
> Official   And it was a black plastic bag, right?
> Customer   Yes.
> Official   And you last saw it on March 20 at two in the afternoon?
> Customer   Yes, in the grocery store.
> Official   And what was in it?
> Customer   All my shopping and my purse.

● 🔊 Play the tape and ask students to check their answers.

SPEAKING

1. **Aim: to practice speaking.**

● Ask the students to work in groups of three or four and to decide where they're likely to hear the sentences.

> **Possible Answers**
> 1. In a drugstore.
> 2. In a clothes store.
> 3. At a Lost and Found office.
> 4. In a doctor's office.
> 5. In a phone booth/At home.

2. **Aim: to practice speaking.**

● Ask the students to match the statements and replies.

> **Answers**
> 1. c   2. b   3. a   4. d   5. e

3. **Aim: to practice speaking.**

● Ask the students to continue one or two of the conversations in writing.

● You may like to ask the students to do this activity for homework.

11

GENERAL COMMENTS

Talking About Obligation

The two modal verbs included here have appeared in earlier lessons, but *can* is used here for permission rather than ability. The main focus is therefore on *have to*, which can be problematic in that the negative, *don't have to*, indicates a lack of obligation rather than a negative obligation. Care should be taken that students don't assume that it is synonymous with *can't*.

Rules and Advice

The rules and advice are presented in the context of traditions and customs in different cultures. None of them are rules in the strict sense of the term, but pieces of strong advice with the suggestion that not following the advice would be as serious as breaking some kind of unwritten law.

VOCABULARY AND READING

1. Aim: to present the words in the vocabulary box; to pre-teach some difficult words.
   ● Ask the students to describe the pictures using the words in the box.

2. Aim: to practice reading for main ideas.
   ● The pictures constitute a form of summary for the rules and advice. The activity is designed to dissuade the students from trying to understand every single word.

LISTENING

1. Aim: to practice listening for main ideas.
   ● Explain to the students that they are going to hear an Australian responding to the statements. At this stage in the course the students should be able to cope with more challenging listening passages. In this listening activity, James comments on all the rules and advice mentioned in the text but the task is graded in such a way that the students are only checking the things mentioned, so that they don't feel they have to understand every word. You could ask the students if they remember one or two of the differences James mentioned, if you feel they are confident, but this is only a gist listening at this stage.

   ● 🎙️ Play the tape.

> **Answers**
> James talks about all the advice and rules mentioned in the text but there are differences in Australia.

2. Aim: to present *don't have to* and *can*.
   ● Most of the rules and advice were not applicable to Australia, so *don't have to* (absence of obligation) and *can* (permission) can be presented.

   ● Ask the students to look at the example sentences and then complete the other sentences.

> **Answers**
> 1. You **don't have to** ask if you want to take a picturegraph of someone.
> 2. You **don't have to** take off your shoes when you go into someone's house.
> 3. You **can** kiss in public.
> 4. You **don't have to** shake hands with everyone when you meet them in Australia. You **can** shake hands when you meet someone for the first time.

3. Aim: to check comprehension; to provide an opportunity for a second listening.
   ● 🎙️ Play the tape and ask the students to listen again and to check their answers.

GRAMMAR

1. Aim: to focus on the difference between *have to* and *don't have to*.

● Ask the students to read the information in the grammar box and then to do the activities.

● Ask the students to do this activity orally.

> **Answers**
> 1. Children **don't have to** be quiet all the time.
> 2. You **have to** be quiet in a library.
> 3. You **have to** go through customs when you enter the United States.
> 4. Men **have to** take off their coats in a church.
> 5. You **don't have to** take off your shoes in an Australian home.
> 6. You **don't have to** wear a uniform to university in the United States.

2. Aim: to practice using *have to, should(n't)*, and *can't* for advice.

● Ask the students to work in pairs and to write some advice for language learners.

● Ask the students to place their advice where the other students can see it.

3. Aim: to practice using *can* and *can't* for rules.

● You may like to ask the students to do this orally in groups.

● Ask each group to tell the rest of the class the rules they have discussed for the school or their place of work.

SPEAKING AND WRITING

1. Aim: to use the target structures; to practice speaking.

● Ask the students to work in pairs and to think of advice and rules they can give to visitors to their country.

2. Aim: to practice writing and speaking.

● To recycle the language covered in 1, ask the students to work with another pair and to draw up a list of advice and rules.

● You may like to ask the students to do the written part of this activity for homework.

12

GENERAL COMMENTS

Present Perfect Tense

This is the first of two lessons in *Move Up* Elementary on the present perfect tense. Although it has an equivalent in form in a number of languages, it is used differently. This lesson focuses on its use to talk about experience.

READING AND VOCABULARY

1. **Aim: to practice speaking; to prepare for reading.**

● The lesson is about visiting San Francisco and other cities with sights to see. Ask the students to make a list of the famous sites to see in their own nearest city.

● Ask the students if they have been to San Francisco. If they have, do they recognize the places in the pictures? Can they think of anything they'd like to see if they went to San Francisco?

2. **Aim: to practice reading for main ideas; to present the present perfect.**

● Ask the students to read the postcard and to say which picture is on the back of it.

> **Answer**
> Cable car

3. **Aim: to check comprehension; to practice reading for specific information.**

● Ask the students to read the postcard again and to check the places Doug and Debbie have been to or the things they've done.

> **Answers**
> ✓ watch a Giants Game
> visit Alcatraz
> ✓ visit Chinatown
> ✓ take a cable car
> ✓ climb Telegraph Hill
> go to the Golden Gate Bridge

4. Aim: to present the words in the vocabulary box.
- Check that the students understand what the words mean. They have already occurred in the lesson, and some of them elsewhere in *Move Up* Elementary.

> **Answers**
> 1. A hill is a small mountain.
> 2. You cross a river by going over a bridge.
> 3. When you climb something, you go up it.
> 4. A park is a public place, with trees and grass.
> 5. The view from a building is what you can see from it.

SOUNDS

1. Aim: to focus on the pronunciation of the present perfect.
- ▭ Play the tape and ask the students to repeat the phrases.

2. Aim: to focus on stressed words in sentences.
- ▭ Play the tape and ask the students to read and listen to the conversation. As they listen, they should underline the stressed syllables. You may need to play the tape several times.

- You can continue this activity by asking the students to write on a separate piece of paper all the words they underlined.

- Then when they're ready, and without looking at their books, they should reconstitute the conversation using the key words as prompts.

> **Answers**
> A Have you ever been to San Francisco?
> B No, I haven't. I've never been there.
> A Have you ever stayed in a hotel?
> B Yes, I have.
> A When was that?
> B When I was in Mexico last year.

3. Aim: to practice speaking.
- Ask the students to practice the conversation in pairs.

- You may like to ask the students to perform the conversation in front of the class.

GRAMMAR

1. Aim: to practice talking about experiences using the present perfect.
- Ask the students to read the information in the grammar box, and then to do the activities.

- Ask the students to work in pairs and to ask and answer questions about Doug and Debbie's vacation. Refer the students back to their answers in *Reading and Vocabulary* activity 3.

2. Aim: to focus on the form of regular past participles.
- Ask the students to look at the past participles and to write the infinitives.

> **Answers**
> live, work, stay, watch, visit, listen

3. Aim: to focus on some irregular past participles.
- Ask the students to do this activity orally in pairs.

> **Answers**
> eat – eaten, drink – drunk, drive – driven,
> read – read, see – seen, fly – flown, take – taken,
> buy – bought, win – won, make – made,
> write – written, send – sent

WRITING

Aim: to practice writing.
- Ask the students to think about a list of places in the city where they are now.

- Ask the students to work alone and to write a postcard to a friend. Ask them to do a first draft.

- Ask the students to show you their first drafts. Make suggestions for improvements and then ask the students to do a second draft.

- You may like to ask students to do this activity for homework.

13

GENERAL COMMENTS

Present Perfect

This is the second use of the present perfect introduced in *Move Up* Elementary, and the one which is likely to give students the greatest difficulty. Many languages use the present simple or the past simple to express actions or states which began in the past and continue now, and students often find it hard to accepte that those tenses cannot perform this function in English. In addition, the use of *for* and *since* to introduce time clauses is often a source of confusion. For this reason, two grammar exercises are devoted to practicing this.

The interview with Abby and Ben Goldman contains examples of natural, conversational English, and you may want to tell students not to try to understand every word they say. The accompanying tasks are graded so that the students are directed to find the main ideas of the interview without having to worry about details.

VOCABULARY AND LISTENING

1. **Aim: to present the words in the vocabulary box; to prepare for listening.**
● Ask the students to look at the picture and read the caption. Make sure they understand who the people are and what they do.

● Ask the students to look at the vocabulary box and predict which words will appear in the interview.

2. **Aim: to read for main ideas; to practice understanding text organization.**
● Ask the students to read the interview and decide where the sentences go.

● Ask the students to check their answers in pairs.

3. **Aim: to practice listening for specific information.**
● 📼 Having read the interview, the students will be ready for this listening activity. Play the tape and ask them to listen and check their answers to 2.

Answers
1. b 2. a 3. d 4. c 5. e

4. **Aim: to practice speaking.**
● Ask the students to work in groups of three and to act out the conversation.

● Ask one or two pairs to perform the conversation in front of the whole class.

GRAMMAR

1. Aim: to practice using the present perfect for unfinished events; to practice using *since* to show the beginning of the event.

● Ask the students to read the information in the grammar box and then to do the activities. You may like to remind them that *since* tells us when the unfinished event began, and so always refers to a point in time rather than a period of time.

● Ask the students to check their answers with another student.

> **Answers**
> 1. (She has worked at the deli) since 1936.
> 2. (He has worked there) since 1946.
> 3. (They have been married) since 1947.
> 4. (They have lived in Brooklyn) since they got married/since 1947.
> 5. (It has been open) since 1922.

2. Aim: to practice using the present perfect for unfinished events; to practice using *for* to show duration.

● Ask the students to rewrite their answers to 1 using *for*. You may like to remind students that *for* tells us how long the action has continued, and so always refers to a period of time.

● Ask the students to check their answers with another student.

> **Answers (in 1997)**
> 1. (She has worked at the deli) for 61 years.
> 2. (He has worked there) for 51 years.
> 3. (They have been married) for 50 years.
> 4. (They have lived in Brooklyn) for 50 years.
> 5. (It has been open) for 75 years.

3. Aim: to check the use of the present perfect tense; to check the use of *for* and *since*.

● Ask the students to do this activity on their own and then to check their answers in pairs.

> **Answers**
> 1. b   2. a   3. a   4. a   5. a   6. b

● Spend some time explaining why these answers are correct.

> 1. b – correct form of present perfect.
> 2. a – this is a completed/finished event in the past, so the past simple is the correct tense.
> 3. a – eight o'clock was when the "action" started, i.e. a specific point in time.
> 4. a – this is a completed/finished action in the past, so the past simple is the correct tense.
> 5. a – present perfect is the correct tense to use to talk about an unfinished event.
> 6. b – present perfect is the correct tense to use to talk about an unfinished event.

SPEAKING AND WRITING

1. Aim: to practice speaking; to prepare for writing.

● Ask students to interview a partner and complete the chart with their partner's information. If your students are not married and have no children, you may like to substitute different headings for the "married" and "children" headings.

2. Aim: to practice writing.

● Ask the students to write a paragraph about their partner, using the information they gathered in 1.

14

GENERAL COMMENTS

Imperatives

Students will have come across imperatives if they have followed *Move Up* Starter, and they will have had passive exposure to imperatives in all the instructions in *Move Up* Elementary. So the structure shouldn't cause the students a great deal of difficulty and for this reason, there are no specific activities in the *Grammar* section.

Picnics

The word *picnic* comes from the French *pique-nique* and was originally used to describe a fashionable social entertainment in which everyone brought food to be shared. Nowadays, it is understood to be a meal, often of cold food, eaten outdoors.

A picnic may be an activity which your students do not do very often, if at all, in their culture. If not, try to choose an equivalent activity, perhaps outdoors, which involves some sharing of food with friends and family for discussion.

SPEAKING

1. Aim: to introduce the theme of the lesson; to practice speaking.
● Ask the students to discuss their idea of a perfect day out. The situations in the textbook are only suggestions.

2. Aim: to practice speaking.
● Ask the students to decide which situation from activity 1 they can see in the picture.

Answer
a picnic in the countryside

READING AND VOCABULARY

1. Aim: to prepare for reading.
● Ask the students to work in pairs and to make a list of things to take on a picnic.

● Ask the students to read out their list. Note down their list of things on the board.

2. Aim: to practice reading for main ideas.
● The drawings represent a summary of each paragraph. If you ask them to do this task, they will be less likely to demand an explanation for difficult vocabulary.

Answers
paragraph 3: trash
paragraph 4: knife, fork
paragraph 5: carton of juice, cups
paragraph 6: blanket
paragraph 7: cooler
paragraph 9: knife, bottle opener, barbeque, matches

3. Aim: to present the words in the vocabulary box.
● The students may not know some of these words. Ask them to try and match the words they know. They will understand the meaning of the other words by a process of elimination.

4. Aim: to practice speaking.
● This activity acknowledges the possibility that students may not have picnics in their country.

● Find out if the kind of picnic described in the passage appeals to the students. Ask them to say where they'd like to have a picnic.

GRAMMAR

1. **Aim: to focus on the infinitive of purpose.**
- Ask the students to read the information in the grammar box and then to do the activities.

- Ask the students to read the passage again and find the answers to these comprehension check questions.

> **Answers**
> 1. **To be** sure there's something to do when you finish your picnic.
> 2. **To avoid** taking knives and forks.
> 3. **To sit** on it or to keep you warm.
> 4. **To keep** it cool.
> 5. **To allow** everyone to carry something.
> 6. **To make** people hungry.

2. **Aim: to practice using the infinitive of purpose; to check comprehension of new vocabulary.**
- Ask the students to do this on their own.

> **Answers**
> 1. fork   2. barbecue   3. knife
> 4. cooler   5. matches   6. blanket

3. **Aim: to practice using the infinitive of purpose; to check comprehension of new vocabulary.**
- Ask the students to check their answers in pairs.

- Check the answers orally with the whole class.

4. **Aim: to practice using the infinitive of purpose.**
- Do this activity with the whole class.

> **Possible Answers**
> 1. To buy food or clothes.
> 2. To relax and visit a foreign country.
> 3. To catch a plane or to meet people.
> 4. To do your job/to learn something and pass your exams.
> 5. To be entertained/to have fun.
> 6. To cut something.

WRITING

1. **Aim: to practice speaking; to prepare for writing.**
- Ask the students to work in groups of two or three. They should decide on one of the suggestions in *Speaking* activity 1. When they have made their decision, they should work alone and make notes on pieces of advice for their chosen outing.

2. **Aim: to practice speaking; to practice writing.**
- Ask the students to put all their ideas together. go around the groups giving extra ideas.

- Ask the students to write their advice in full sentences using the imperative and *to* + infinitive.

- You may like to ask the students to do this writing activity for homework.

3. **Aim: to practice speaking.**
- Ask the students to show their advice to other students and to discuss it.

- If it's suitable, you may like to put their advice on the wall for everyone to see.

15

GENERAL COMMENTS

Adverbs

The students will already have come across some adverbs of time, such as *often* and *sometimes*, in Book A, Lesson 11. This lesson gives a very brief introduction to adverbs of manner. There are many other issues concerning adverbs which are not covered in *Move Up* Elementary: the position of adverbs of time, manner, and place; adjectives which look like adverbs (such as *friendly*), full coverage of adverbs with the same form as the adjective (*fast, high, low, wide*). These are all covered in later levels of the *Move Up* series.

School

This lesson has school as its theme, which lends itself to showing adverbs of manner in a suitable context. If your students are still in school, they should be encouraged to think about their early schooldays and to see if there is a difference in their attitude and behavior between then and now.

The theme of the lesson concerns school performance and later success in life.

VOCABULARY

1. **Aim: to present the words in the vocabulary box.**
● Ask the students to match the adverbs with their opposites. You may like to do this activity orally with the whole class.

Answers
badly – well, carefully – carelessly, quickly – slowly, loudly – quietly, politely – rudely

2. **Aim: to check comprehension of the new words; to practice listening to tone of voice.**
● 🔊 Play the tape and ask the students to say how the four people are speaking.

Answers
Conversation 1: quietly
Conversation 2: rudely
Conversation 3: politely
Conversation 4: loudly

READING AND SPEAKING

1. **Aim: to prepare for reading; to practice speaking.**
● Ask the students to look at the pictures and to say what the people do.

Answers
doctor
musician
athlete
business woman

2. **Aim: to prepare for reading.**
● Ask the students to say what their teacher said about them when they were in high school.

3. **Aim: to practice reading for main ideas.**
● Tell your students that the reading passage is made up of extracts from high school report cards. Do the extracts look like their own high school report cards?

● Ask the students to read the report cards and to match the adult in the picture with the child in the report.

Answers
first picture: Trudy
second picture: Antonia
third picture: Carlos
fourth picture: Kate

4. **Aim: to check comprehension.**
● Ask the students to say what each student was good at.

Answers
Antonia was good at music and art.
Carlos was good at sports.
Trudy was good at math and biology.
Kate was good at French and English.

5. **Aim: to practice speaking.**
● Ask the students to talk about the subjects they were good at. Are they still good at these subjects?

GRAMMAR

1. Aim: to focus on the formation of adverbs.

● Ask the students to read the information in the grammar box and then to do the activities.

● Do this activity with the whole class. Write the answers on the board.

> **Answers**
> badly – bad, carefully – careful, carelessly – careless, quickly – quick, loudly – loud, politely – polite, quietly – quiet, rudely – rude, slowly – slow, well – good

2. Aim: to focus on the formation of adverbs.

● Ask the students to do this activity on their own and then correct it with the whole class.

> **Answers**
> angrily, happily, gently, immediately, successfully, comfortably, suddenly, dangerously, frequently

3. Aim: to focus on the distinction between adjectives and adverbs.

● Remind the students that an adverb is used to describe a verb, and an adjective is used to describe a noun.

● Ask the students to complete the sentences on their own.

> **Answers**
> 1. He spoke **clearly** so everyone could hear him **well**.
> 2. They were late so they had a **quick** game of handball and then left.
> 3. She had a very **successful** class with her students.
> 4. He listened to his teacher very **carefully**.
> 5. Could you speak more **slowly**, please? Your accent is **hard** to understand.
> 6. He passed the oral exam very **easily**.

4. Aim: to practice speaking; to practice using adverbs.

● Ask the students to talk about what other students can do and how well they can do it.

LISTENING AND SPEAKING

1. Aim: to prepare for listening.

● Ask the students to read the questions about school and to think about their answers.

● You may like to ask a few students for their feedback.

2. Aim: to practice listening for main ideas.

● 🔲 Play the tape and ask the students to listen and to check the statements the speakers say *yes* to.

● Explain that the students may not understand every word, but they should understand enough to perform the task.

3. Aim: to practice speaking; to check comprehension.

● Ask the students to check their answers in pairs. Ask them to try to remember exactly what the speakers say.

● 🔲 Play the tape again.

> **Answers**
>
> | | Joel | Patrice |
> |---|---|---|
> | Do/did you always work very hard? | ✓ | ✓ |
> | Do/did you always listen carefully to your teachers? | ✗ | ✗ |
> | Do/did you always behave very well ? | ✗ | ✓ |
> | Do/did you pass your tests easily? | ✗ | ✗ |
> | Do/did you always write slowly and carefully? | ✓ | ✓ |
> | Do/did you think schooldays are/were the best days of your life? | ✗ | ✗ |

4. Aim: to practice speaking.

● Ask the students to ask and answer the questions and to check the statements they say *yes* to.

● You may like to ask some students what their answers were.

Progress Check 11–15

GENERAL COMMENTS

You can work through this Progress Check in the order shown, or concentrate on areas which have caused difficulty in Lessons 11 to 15. You can also let the students choose the activities they would like or feel the need to do.

VOCABULARY

1. Aim: to focus on collocations.

● There has already been quite a lot of work on collocations in *Move Up* Elementary, but the students have not yet used the specific terms.

● Ask the students to think of other words which go with the adjectives.

Possible Answers
cold day, weather
difficult exam, time
low land, bridge
old lady, man
expensive holiday, car

2. Aim: to focus on English outside the classroom.

● Encourage the students to think of all the different places outside the classroom where they can see and listen to English. The list in this activity isn't exhaustive, but it's designed to demonstrate to the students that even in small towns there may be opportunities to come across examples of English.

GRAMMAR

1. Aim: to review *should(n't)* and *have to*.

Answers
1. should   2. have to   3. shouldn't
4. shouldn't   5. have to   6. shouldn't

2. Aim: to review the infinitive of purpose.

Answers
1. to keep warm
2. to go swimming
3. to go shopping
4. to light something
5. to open a bottle
6. to speak to someone (a long way away)

3. Aim: to review the formation of adverbs.

Answers
easily, well, carefully, fast, hard, politely, quietly, rudely

4. Aim: to review the distinction between adjectives and adverbs.

Answers
1. well   2. fast   3. polite   4. quiet   5. hard   6. easily

SOUNDS

1. Aim: to focus on /eə/ and /ɪə/.
- Remind the students once again that the relationship between spelling and pronunciation in English is not as close as in other languages.

- Ask the students to group the words according to the diphthongs.

> **Answers**
> /ɪə/: beer, near, hear, we're, year
> /eə/: stair, hair, chair, air

- 🔲 Play the tape and ask the students to say the words out loud.

2. Aim: to focus on /əʊ/ and /ɔː/.
- These are two very difficult phonemes for most students, so don't expect them to pronounce them correctly.

> **Answers**
> /əʊ/: so, Jo, go, low, toe
> /ɔː/: tore, war, floor, sore, sport

- 🔲 Play the tape. As they listen, ask the students to say the words out loud.

3. Aim: to focus on stressed words and their effect on meaning.
- Explain that the speaker will stress the word he or she thinks is important, and this will influence the meaning of the whole sentence.

- 🔲 Play the tape and ask the students simply to read and follow the tapescript.

- You may like to ask the students to practice the exchanges in pairs.

READING

1. Aim: to prepare for reading.
- Ask the students to look at the pictures and predict what happens in the story.

- Ask the students to read the story and check the predictions.

2. Aim: to focus on word order.
- Ask the students to cross out unnecessary words, i.e. words which can be left out without creating a syntactical error or without changing the meaning.

- You may need to explain the meaning of any difficult words.

3. Aim: to check the answer to 2.
- Ask the students to work in pairs and to check their answers.

- Find out how many words the students have crossed out.

> **Possible Answers**
> A ~~young~~ man went into a ~~local~~ bank, went ~~up~~ to the ~~woman~~ teller and gave her a note and a ~~plastic~~ bag. The note said, "Put ~~all~~ your money into this bag, ~~please~~." The ~~middle-aged~~ teller was ~~very~~ frightened so she gave him ~~all~~ the money. He put it in his bag and ran out of the ~~front~~ door. When he got ~~back~~ home the ~~city~~ police were there. His note was on an old, ~~white~~ envelope and on the envelope was his ~~home~~ address.

4. Aim: to focus on word order.
- You will find that most texts will contain some "unnecessary" words. If, by some unlucky chance, the text chosen does not contain unnecessary words, even the process of looking for them will be a worthwhile activity.

- You may like to ask your students to do this activity for homework.

16

GENERAL COMMENTS

Future Simple

This is the first of two lessons in which the future simple is presented. At this level, the students are not expected to be able to use this tense expertly. They simply need to know how it is formed, which is relatively straightforward, and its two principle uses: to talk about a decision made at the time of speaking (Lesson 16) and to make predictions (Lesson 17). Further work on the future simple and its uses is provided in later levels of the *Move Up* series.

VOCABULARY AND SOUNDS

1. Aim: to present the words in the box.
- Ask the students to look at the words, and to check that they understand them. Ask other students to explain the meaning of the words, if necessary.

- Write *ship* and *plane* on the board. Ask the students to come up in turn and to write a word in the correct column. Some words can go in both columns.

Answers
ship: passport control, port, on board, cruise, first class, travel agency
plane: departure lounge, passport control, baggage reclaim, check-in, arrival hall, boarding pass, business class, first class, round-trip, one-way, departure gate, economy class

2. Aim: to practice pronouncing two-word nouns.
- 🔊 Play the tape and ask the students to underline the stressed word.

Answers
<u>departure</u> lounge, <u>passport</u> control, <u>business</u> class, <u>travel</u> agency, <u>arrival</u> hall

- Ask the students to say the words out loud.

LISTENING

1. Aim: to prepare for listening; to practice reading for main ideas; to present the future simple.
- Ask the students to read the conversation and to say where it takes place.

Answer
At a travel agency.

2. Aim: to practice listening for specific information.
- 🔊 Play the tape and ask the students to listen and underline anything which is different from what they hear.

Answers
A May I help you?
B Yes, I need a flight to <u>Miami</u>.
A One-way or round-trip?
B Round-trip.
A When do you want to travel? It's cheaper if you spend <u>Sunday</u> night in <u>Miami</u>.
B I'll go on Thursday and come back on <u>Tuesday</u>, then.
A And will that be economy or business class?
B Oh, I'll take <u>economy</u> class, please.
A OK, that's going to be <u>$199.87</u>. How would you like to pay?
B Do you take checks?
A No, ma'am, only credit cards.
B OK, I'll use my <u>American Express</u> card, then. Oh, can you arrange a rental car for me at the airport?
A Yes, of course. We can get you a small car for <u>$34.50</u> a day.
B Perfect! For <u>five</u> days then.
A So, that'll be <u>$372.37</u> total.
B Thanks.

- Ask the students to check their answers in pairs.

GRAMMAR

1. Aim: to practice using the future simple.

● Ask the students to read the information in the grammar box, and then to do the activities.

● Draw the students' attention to the future simple in the conversation and explain that it's used when you talk about a decision at the moment of speaking.

● Divide the students into pairs of Student A and Student B. Ask each student to change some details in the conversation.

2. Aim: to practice speaking.

● Ask the students to act out the conversation when they're ready.

● You may like to ask the students to act out their conversations in front of the class.

READING AND SPEAKING

1. Aim: to practice reading for main ideas.

● Ask the students if they would like to go to the Caribbean. Ask them what they would like to do or see there. Find out if anyone has already been there.

● Ask the students to read the travel brochure and to follow the route on the map.

Answers
Maimi to San Juan, Puerto Rico
San Juan to Antigua
Antigua to Barbados
Barbados to Trinidad and Tobago
Trinidad to Curaçao
Curaçao to Aruba
Aruba to Jamaica
Jamaica to Miami

2. Aim: to practice reading for specific information; to check comprehension.

● This activity provides an opportunity for a closer look at the text. You may want to explain a few words, but by now, the students should be able to accept that they won't be able to understand every single word.

Answers
1. Ten days.
2. Two days.
3. No.
4. By plane.
5. Yes, at an additional charge.
6. Yes.
7. Travel insurance and on-island transport.
8. No.

3. Aim: to practice reading and speaking.

● The Communication Activities contain extra information for a role play between tourists and tour organizers.

● Ask the students to read the relevant Communication Activity and to act out the role play.

● You may like to ask the students to write out their role plays and learn them for homework. At the start of the next lesson you can ask some of them to perform their role plays to the rest of the class.

17

GENERAL COMMENTS

The Weather

This lesson covers some very simple vocabulary to describe the weather. You may want to add extra words to describe the weather in the place where you're teaching at the moment.

In our research for *Move Up*, we have found that despite the importance of the topic, many teachers and students are less willing than perhaps they were to discuss environmental matters. This is possibly because it is a subject which is covered extensively in newspapers and other media. It may also be that it is a subject which is not discussed a great deal outside the classroom. You may want to be vigilant of spending too much time on a topic which, while it constitutes an important lexical field, may not maintain the interest of the students.

VOCABULARY AND LISTENING

1. **Aim: to present the words in the vocabulary box.**
- Teach the meaning of the words by asking the students to match them with the weather symbols.

- You may need to explain some of the symbols if they represent weather with which the students are unfamiliar.

Answers
fog, snow, wind, cloud, sun, rain

2. **Aim: to present the words in the vocabulary box.**
- You may need to translate or illustrate these words in some way if your students come from a country which doesn't have these extremes of weather.

3. **Aim: to practice saying what the weather is like.**
- Ask the students to say what the weather is like in the pictures.

- Ask the students to say what the weather is like today, and what it was like yesterday.

- Try to match some of the words with different months or seasons of the year. You may also like to bring some magazine pictures of different outdoor scenes from different countries to illustrate the words. If you can collect enough to illustrate each word, hand out the pictures and ask the students to go around saying *What's the weather like?* and eliciting a reply which is appropriate to the weather in the picture.

4. **Aim: to practice listening for specific information.**
- ▭ Play the weather forecast and ask the students to underline anything which is different from what they hear.

Answers
And here's the weather forecast for the world's major cities. Athens, cloudy and 54 degrees. Bangkok, cloudy and 86 degrees. Cairo, sunny and 61 degrees. Geneva, cloudy and 50 degrees. Hong Kong, cloudy and 68 degrees. Istanbul, rainy and 44 degrees. Kuala Lumpur, sunny and 95 degrees. Lisbon, cloudy and 52 degrees. Madrid, rainy and 44 degrees. Moscow, snowy and 14 degrees. New York, sunny and 32 degrees. Paris, snowy and 21 degrees. Prague, sunny and 28 degrees. Rio, cloudy and 20 degrees. Rome, rainy and 48 degrees. Tokyo, snowy and 24 degrees and finally Warsaw, cloudy and 17 degrees.

- You may like to spend some time asking the students to say what country the different cities are in.

GRAMMAR

1. **Aim: to focus on the form of the future simple for predictions.**
- Ask the students to read the information in the grammar box and then to do the activities.

- Remind the students that the two meanings of the future simple presented in *Move Up* Elementary are decisions made at the moment of speaking (Lesson 16) and predictions (Lesson 17).

- This is a fairly mechanical, drill-like activity, but at least it will give the students plenty of opportunity of using the future simple and the words for describing the weather. You may like to check their answers with the whole class.

2. Aim: to practice using comparative forms of the adjectives in the vocabulary box; to practice using the future simple for predictions.

● Ask the students to make comparisons between the two towns.

> **Possible Answers**
> 1. It'll be hotter in Cairo than in Tokyo.
> 2. It'll be hotter in Athens than in Rome.
> 3. It'll be colder in Moscow than in Warsaw.
> 4. It'll be hotter in Bangkok than in Lisbon.
> 5. It'll be colder in Prague than in Madrid.
> 6. It'll be colder in Istanbul than in Athens.

3. Aim: to practice the future simple for predictions.

● Ask the students to write a short forecast for tomorrow.

● Find out if everyone has made similar predictions.

READING AND SPEAKING

1. Aim: to practice using the target structures; to prepare for reading.

● Ask the students to look at the predictions about the weather in twenty-five years and to decide if they're true for their country.

● Check the students' predictions with the whole class.

2. Aim: to practice reading for main ideas and for specific information.

● The predictions in 1 constitute a framework for the main ideas of the text. Although the students will read the text for specific information, they will also get a clear picture of the text's main ideas as a whole.

> **Answers**
> | | |
> |---|---|
> | It'll be colder. | False |
> | The sea level will be lower. | False |
> | It'll be windier. | True |
> | It'll be wetter. | True, in the Midwest |
> | There'll be more snow. | False |

3. Aim: to prepare for listening; to practice speaking.

● Ask the students to discuss these predictions, either in small groups or with the whole class.

4. Aim: to practice speaking; to practice using the target structures.

● Ask the students to continue the discussion in groups of two or three. Ask them to make predictions about the following: *population, medical research, the economy, politics, transport.*

● Ask the students to tell other students about their predictions. How many groups made similar predictions?

18

GENERAL COMMENTS

Active and Passive

The passive voice is introduced for the first time in this lesson. The form of the passive is straightforward. You use the various tenses of the verb *to be* + past participle. However, the full range of uses are not so easy to explain. This lesson restricts itself to the way the passive allows you to shift the focus from the object of an active verb to the subject. The other uses are covered more fully in later levels of *Move Up*.

The Round-the-World Quiz

The quiz in this lesson assumes that the students have a certain level of general knowledge. The questions are as simple as possible and drawn from a wide geographical and cultural background. However, it doesn't matter if the students have difficulty in answering them. The primary aim of the lesson is to introduce the passive. Testing the students' general knowledge is of secondary importance.

SPEAKING AND VOCABULARY

1. Aim: to practice speaking.

● As a warm-up for the rest of the lesson, which involves a general knowledge quiz, ask the students to read the statements and say if they are true.

● You may like to check the students' answers with the whole class, or if you think they may have difficulty getting the correct answers, you may decide to give them the answers without finding out who got them right.

Answers
The sentences are all meant to be true, although some of claims have been disputed (Shakespeare, Marconi).

2. Aim: to present the words in the vocabulary box.

● These words are among the most common ones to be used in the passive. They will therefore be useful later in the lesson.

● Remind the students that the sentences in 1 were true. They should be able to transfer the meaning of the new vocabulary to complete the sentences in this activity.

Answers
1. painted 2. grow 3. discovered 4. built
5. wrote 6. make 7. invented 8. composed

READING

1. Aim: to practice reading for specific information.

● Ask the students to read *The Round-the-World Quiz* and to check the correct answers.

2. Aim: to practice speaking; to check comprehension.

● Ask the students to check their answers in pairs.

● You shouldn't give them the correct answers at this stage, because this will detract from the value of the *Listening* activity.

GRAMMAR

1. Aim: to focus on the form of the passive.

● Ask the students to read the information in the grammar box and then to do the activities.

● Ask the students to check how the passive is formed. Tell them that there are other tenses which are used in the passive, but in this lesson, only the present and the past passive are covered.

Answers
Sentences 1–7: present passive
Sentences 8–15: past passive

2. Aim: to focus on the form of the passive.

● This transformation activity from the passive back to the active should give the students further help in understanding how the passive is formed. Make sure they use *they* in the present active sentences.

● You may like to check the answers with the whole class.

Answers
They grow coffee in Brazil.
They make Daewoo cars in Korea.
They make Sony computers in Japan.
They grow tea in India.
They grow tobacco in the U.S.A.
They make Benetton clothes in Italy.
They make Roquefort cheese in France.
The Americans invented the atom bomb.
Picasso painted *Guernica*.
Christopher Columbus discovered the Caribbean islands.
Bell invented the telephone.
Shakespeare wrote *Romeo and Juliet*.
Sultan Ahmet built the Blue Mosque.
Paul McCartney composed *Yesterday*.
The Pharaohs built the Pyramids.

3. Aim: to practice writing the passive.

● By now, the formation of the passive should be causing few problems. Ask the students to rewrite the sentences in *Speaking and Vocabulary* activity 2 in the passive.

● Once again, you may like to correct this activity with the whole class.

Answers
1. *La Primavera* was painted by Botticelli.
2. Oranges are grown in Florida.
3. Radioactivity was discovered by Marie Curie.
4. The Taj Mahal was built by Shah Jehan.
5. The *Odyssey* was written by Homer.
6. Honda cars are built in Japan.
7. Gunpowder was invented by the Chinese.
8. The *1812 Symphony* was composed by Tchaikovsky.

LISTENING

1. Aim: to practice listening for main ideas.

● Having done the quiz, the students should be well-prepared for this listening activity. Remind them that they don't have to understand everything that Frank and Sally say, only their answers.

● 🔲 Play the tape.

Correct Answers
1. Brazil 2. Korea 3. Japan 4. India
5. the U.S.A. 6. Italy 7. France 8. the Americans
9. Picasso 10. Christopher Columbus 11. Bell
12. Shakespeare 13. Sultan Ahmet 14. Paul McCartney 15. The Pharaohs

Frank and Sally scored 14.

2. Aim: to check the students' answers to *Reading* activity 2.

● Ask the students to check their own score of correct answers.

WRITING AND SPEAKING

1. Aim: to practice writing.

● Ask the students to work in pairs and to write a few quiz questions. Ask them to think of one correct and two incorrect answers to each question.

● You may like to ask them to do this activity for homework.

2. Aim: to practice reading.

● Collect the quizzes and give them out to new pairs. Ask the new pair to do the quiz.

19

GENERAL COMMENTS

Reported Speech

In this lesson, a very brief presentation of reported speech is given, in which only the tense shift from present simple to past simple is given. Students will be given more extensive coverage of reported speech, reported questions, and reporting verbs in *Move Up* Intermediate and Upper Intermediate.

Youth Hostels

You may like to explain that youth hostels are cheap forms of accommodation, both for teenagers and for families. In the United States, youth hostels have existed for many years, but have been slow in gaining popularity, perhaps because there are many excellent campsites.

LISTENING AND READING

1. **Aim: to prepare for listening; to practice understanding text organization.**
- Ask the students to read the conversation and to decide where the sentences go.
- Ask the students to check their answers with another student.

2. **Aim: to practice listening for specific information.**
- ▣ Having read the conversation the students will be ready for this listening activity. Play the tape and ask them to listen and check their answers to 1.

> **Answers**
> 1. e   2. d   3. a   4. c   5. b

3. **Aim: to practice reading for specific information; to prepare the presentation of reported speech.**
- This activity involves some close reading of the brochure and the conversation.
- Ask the students to read the brochure and the conversation and to underline any information which is different.

> **Answers**
>
> | | |
> |---|---|
> | CHRIS | Good afternoon. |
> | RECEPTIONIST | Hi there! Can I help you? |
> | CHRIS | Do you have any beds for tonight? |
> | RECEPTIONIST | Yes, I think so. You see, I've just started work at the hostel. How long would you like to stay? |
> | CHRIS | We'll stay for just one night. |
> | RECEPTIONIST | Yes, that's OK. |
> | TONY | Great! |
> | RECEPTIONIST | How old are you? |
> | TONY | We're both sixteen. |
> | RECEPTIONIST | OK, that'll be $13 each. |
> | CHRIS | Is it far from the hostel to Eureka? |
> | RECEPTIONIST | No, not really, it's two miles. It takes about an hour on foot. |
> | TONY | Is there a bus? |
> | RECEPTIONIST | I think so. It takes about fifteen minutes. There's a bus every hour. |
> | TONY | What time is the last bus from Eureka? |
> | RECEPTIONIST | I think it leaves at nine o'clock. There's not much to do at night. |
> | CHRIS | We're exhausted! We need to go to bed early. What time does the hostel close in the morning? |
> | RECEPTIONIST | Umm, at eleven A.M. Where are you walking to? |
> | CHRIS | We're going to Crescent City. Are you serving dinner tonight? |
> | RECEPTIONIST | Yes, we're serving dinner until eight o'clock. And breakfast starts at seven thirty. |
> | TONY | And where's the nearest campsite? |
> | RECEPTIONIST | I'm not sure. I think it's Fortuna, which is about ten miles north of here. I started work last Monday so I'm very new here. |

4. Aim: to present reported speech.

● This exchange focuses on the tense shift which reported speech requires.

● 📼 Play the tape. Ask the students to put the parts of the conversation below in the order they hear them. Don't spend too long on this as the text organization aspect of the activity is less important than the presentation of reported speech.

> **Answers**
> 1. CHRIS It's very strange. She said one night cost $13, but it costs $12.
> 2. TONY Yes, and she said it was two miles to Eureka.
> 3. CHRIS But, in fact, it's three miles.
> 4. TONY And she said the last bus left at nine o'clock. But it leaves at eight o'clock.

GRAMMAR

1. Aim: to focus on the tense shift and pronoun change in reported speech.

● Ask the students to read the information in the grammar box and then to do the activities.

● Do this activity orally with the whole class. Ask the students to look back at the transcript of the conversation.

> **Answers**
> 1. "We're both sixteen," said Tony.
> 2. "It takes an hour on foot," said the receptionist.
> 3. "There's a bus every hour," said the receptionist.
> 4. "There isn't much to do at night," said the receptionist.
> 5. "We're exhausted," said Chris.
> 6. "We need to go to bed early," said Chris.

2. Aim: to focus on the tense shift in reported speech; to listen to the conversation in *Listening and Reading* 4; to provide material for writing the letter of complaint.

● This activity performs a variety of functions. Ask the students to look at the rest of the conversation and to complete it.

● You may like to ask the students to check this in pairs.

● Ask several students to perform the conversation to the rest of the class.

> **Answers**
> CHRIS And she said the bus **took** fifteen minutes. But in fact, it takes **ten** minutes.
> TONY And she said the hostel **closed** at eleven A.M., but it's open all day.
> CHRIS The brochure says that they **serve** dinner from six to seven.
> TONY But she said they were serving until eight o'clock. And she also said breakfast **started** at seven thirty...
> CHRIS ... when, in fact, it says here that breakfast **starts** at seven.
> TONY And she said that Fortuna **was** ten miles away, but it **isn't**. It's eight miles away.
> CHRIS And she said that Fortuna **was** north of here. But **it's** south of here!

3. Aim: to check activity 2; to practice listening for specific information.

● 📼 Play the tape and ask the students to check their answers to 2.

VOCABULARY AND WRITING

1. Aim: to present the words in the vocabulary box.

● Ask the students to check that they know what the words mean. Ask them to look for the words in the sentences they first saw them.

2. Aim: to practice writing.

● Ask the students to complete the letter using reported speech and as many of the words in the vocabulary box as possible.

● You may like to ask the students to do this activity for homework.

20

GENERAL COMMENTS

Tense Review

This final teaching lesson uses a story to review all the tenses presented in *Move Up* Elementary.

Stories and Readers

Most students enjoy stories and if they are happy to read or listen to them, they should usually be left to enjoy them. The activities set in this story are designed not so much to test comprehension but to help the students understand the story better. It's also important to break up longer stories so the students are not daunted by long blocks of text. This story is in five parts, each with different activities.

Dear Ruth ... Love Jan comes from the Elementary level of the *Heinemann Guided Readers*. In this lesson it is in a shortened form, and if your students enjoy the story they may enjoy the longer version. There are other stories at a suitable level in this series, and you may want to encourage your students to do some extensive reading using this source of material.

GRAMMAR

1. Aim: to review the tenses and their forms.

● Ask the students to read the information in the grammar box and then to do the activities.

● There should be no surprises for the students in this activity, so you may like to do it quickly with the whole class.

> **Answers**
> 1. b   2. c   3. a   4. d   5. e

2. Aim: to focus on the tenses and their uses.

● Explain that one tense may have more than one use.

● Ask the students to do this activity on their own and then to check it with another student.

● Check the answers with the whole class.

> **Answers**
> a. present perfect
> b. present continuous
> c. future simple
> d. present simple
> e. past simple
> f. present perfect
> g. future simple

READING AND LISTENING

1. Aim: to focus on text type; to prepare for reading.

● Explain that there may be a lot of information to be gained from looking at the illustrations and establishing the text type. This may eventually help them to get a better picture of the main idea of the story.

> **Answer**
> a love story

2. Aim: to prepare for reading; to pre-teach difficult vocabulary.

● In fact, this vocabulary may not be too difficult, but as it is contained in the first part of the story and needs to be clear for the students to understand this first part, it is better to pre-teach it. Ask students to explain any words which others find difficult before you explain it yourself.

● Ask the students to work in pairs and to predict what the first part of the story is about.

● Ask several pairs to give feedback to the rest of the class.

3. **Aim: to practice reading for main ideas.**
- Ask the students to read the first part of the story and to check their answers to 2.
- Did everyone predict correctly?

4. **Aim: to prepare for reading.**
- Once again, ask the students to predict what the next part of the story is likely to be about.

5. **Aim: to practice reading for main ideas.**
- Ask the students to read the next part of the story. Did they predict correctly in 4?

Answers
1. yes
2. to the park/to a coffee shop
3. her ex-boyfriend
4. go outside
5. yes

6. **Aim: to prepare for listening.**
- Ask the students to say what they think Ruth's parents will be like. Do they think her parents will approve of Jan?
- Ask the students to decide who they think is speaking. It will be difficult to distinguish at this stage between Mr. and Mrs. Clark, but the recording will make it clear.
- 🔲 Play the tape and ask them to check.

Answers
1. Jan 2. Jan 3. Ruth 4. Mrs. Clark
5. Mrs. Clark 6. Ruth 7. Ruth

7. **Aim: to prepare for listening.**
- Ask the students to say what will happen next.
- At this stage, it is to be hoped that the students will be enjoying the story. As a result, the preparation work doesn't need to take so much time as in earlier stages of this lesson, and the tasks set while listening and reading do not need to be so elaborate or supportive.

8. **Aim: to practice reading for main ideas.**
- Ask the students to turn to the Communication Activity for the next part of the story.

9. **Aim: to predict the ending of the story.**
- Ask the students to say if the story has a happy or a sad ending. Ask them also if they have enjoyed the story so far.
- Ask the students to turn to the Communication Activity as instructed, if they would like to know the ending of the story.

VOCABULARY AND WRITING

1. **Aim: to check comprehension of the words in the vocabulary box.**
- Ask the students to check that they understand the words and to try and remember where they first saw them.

2. **Aim: to practice writing.**
- Ask the students to write a different ending to the story. There are many places where their ending could begin. It could begin, for example, after Jan meets Ruth's parents.
- You may like to ask the students to do this activity for homework.
- Ask the students to read out their endings to the rest of the class.

Progress Check 16–20

GENERAL COMMENTS

You can work through this Progress Check in the order shown, or concentrate on areas which have caused difficulty in Lessons 16 to 20. You can also let the students choose the activities they would like or feel the need to do.

VOCABULARY

1. Aim: to focus on prepositions after verbs.
- The students will have come across prepositions of time and place. They will also have noticed some multi-part verbs, i.e. verbs which have more than one word. Without going into the complex area of phrasal verbs, this activity focuses on some of the important verbs which are followed by a preposition.

- Ask the students to match the verbs and the prepositions. Explain that some verbs may go with more than one preposition.

> **Answers**
> apologize for/to, belong to, complain about, hear about/of, insist on, pay for, talk to/about/with, think about, worry about

2. Aim: to review vocabulary and topics.
- Remind the students that recording new words under the topics they belong to will be helpful when they need to review them.

- Ask the students to review the vocabulary they have come across in *Move Up* Elementary by asking them to think of or to find words which go under the topic headings suggested. They may find the Map of the Book helpful.

3. Aim: to practice talking; to review vocabulary.
- Ask the students to check their answers to 2 in pairs.

GRAMMAR

1. Aim: to review the future simple for decisions.
- Ask the students to write sentences saying what they'll do in the situations mentioned. Remind them to use the future simple.

> **Possible Answers**
> 1. I'll go shopping.
> 2. I'll go to bed.
> 3. I'll go to the doctor.
> 4. I'll look it up in the dictionary.
> 5. I'll ask a friend to give me some.
> 6. I'll call him.

2. Aim: to review the future simple for predictions.
- Ask the students to make their own predictions about the things mentioned.

3. Aim: to review the passive.

> **Answers**
> 1. The Sistine Chapel was painted by Michelangelo.
> 2. Cotton is grown in Egypt.
> 3. Mercedes cars are made in Germany.
> 4. *The Old Man and the Sea* was written by Hemingway.
> 5. *Aida* was composed by Verdi.
> 6. The Statue of Liberty was built by the French.

4. Aim: to review reported speech.

> **Answers.**
> 1. He said he was sick.
> 2. She said it closed at seven.
> 3. She said it left in five minutes.
> 4. He said he worked in an office.
> 5. They said they lived in New York.
> 6. He said she went shopping on Saturday.

5. Aim: to review the tenses presented in *Move Up* Elementary.
- Ask the students to write true sentences about themselves using all the tenses.

SOUNDS

1. **Aim: to focus on /ɔː/ and /ɔɪ/.**

● Write the two phonemes on the board.

● Say the words out loud and ask students to come and write the words on the board.

> **Answers**
> /ɔɪ/: toy, boy, noise
> /ɔː/: tore, bore, sore, door, war, more

● 🔊 Play the tape and ask the students to listen and check.

● Point out the different spelling of the two sounds.

2. **Aim: to focus on stressed syllables in words.**

● Write the words on the board.

● Ask students to come to the board and underline the stressed syllable.

> **Answers**
> in<u>vent</u>, com<u>pose</u>, dis<u>cover</u>, <u>adult</u>,
> <u>travel</u>, di<u>rector</u>, <u>foreigner</u>, for<u>get</u>

● 🔊 Play the tape and ask the students to repeat the words.

3. **Aim: to focus on stressed words in sentences.**

● Remind the students that the speaker will stress the words that he or she considers to be important.

● 🔊 Play the tape and ask the students to underline the stressed words. You may need to play the tape several times.

> **Answer**
> A <u>young</u> <u>man</u> arrived at J.F.K. <u>airport</u>. His <u>name</u> was
> <u>Jan Polanski</u> and he came from <u>Poland</u>. He was in
> the <u>United States</u> for a <u>course</u> at an <u>English language</u>
> <u>school</u>. He took a <u>cab</u> to the <u>Modern Language</u>
> <u>Institute</u>, went <u>inside</u>, and <u>met</u> the <u>director</u>.

● Ask the students to read the passage out loud. Make sure they stress the correct words.

SPEAKING

Aim: to review all the language presented in *Move Up* Elementary.

● This is designed to be a light-hearted end to the whole course. You may want to make enlarged copies of this page.

● Make sure you bring a few counters and some dice to class.

● You may like to encourage the groups to race against each other. So the first person to finish wins in the group, and the first group to finish wins in the class.

Communication Activities

1 *Progress check 16–20*

Speaking

Now play
*Move Up
Snakes and
Ladders.*

FINISH **Progress Check**	**40** Where's Jan staying? Have Ruth's parents met many foreigners?	**39** Where is Jan from? Why is he in the United States?	**38** What facilities does the youth hostel have?	**37** When are the meals at the youth hostel?	**36** Who wrote *Hamlet*? Name another play written by this person.
31 You need to get to New York quickly. What will you do?	**32** Can you name three islands in the Caribbean? Have you ever been on a cruise?	**33** What will the weather be like tomorrow?	**34** Make a prediction for the future.	**35** Where is coffee grown? What is grown in your country?	**Progress Check**
Progress Check	**30** What were you good at in high school? *or* What places can you see and listen to English?	**29** How did Trudy pass her exam? How does Antonia play the guitar?	**28** What's your advice for a perfect day out?	**27** What is your idea of a perfect day out?	**26** How long have Ben and Abby been married? How long have you studied English?
21 What can you or can't you do in your English class?	**22** What advice can you give to visitors to your country?	**23** Have you ever been to San Francisco? Have you ever stayed in a hotel?	**24** What is the most interesting place you have ever visited?	**25** What is a deli? Would you like to visit New York?	**Progress Check**
Progress Check	**20** What do you think is the most exciting sport? And the most dangerous sport?	**19** What's your favorite sport?	**18** Compare your country with another country?	**17** Is Brazil smaller than the U.S.? Is your country colder than the U.S.?	**16** What number do you call in a medical emergency? Why do you call this number?
11 Do you usually go shopping by yourself?	**12** Name four things you buy as gifts for other people?	**13** What does your friend look like? Describe him/her.	**14** What's Joan's purse made of? When did she lose it?	**15** Name three parts of the body.	**Progress Check**
Progress Check	**10** What is a *doggy bag*? What does a waitress do?	**9** What would you like to eat? Do you like spaghetti?	**8** What's Andrew going to do in the New Year? What's your New Year's resolution?	**7** What are you going to do this weekend?	**6** Name four items of clothing.
1 What is the name of Agatha Christie's famous detective?	**2** Why did Agatha Christie disappear?	**3** When is New Year's Day? When is your birthday?	**4** How do you say *July 10* and *October 31*?	**5** What's Erin doing? What are you wearing?	**Progress Check**
START					

2 *Lesson 2*

Speaking, activity 2

Pair A: Rewrite these facts as quiz questions.

1. The Kobe earthquake was in 1995.
2. Martin Luther King died in 1968.
3. Alexander Graham Bell invented the telephone.
4. Michelangelo was 88 years old when he died.
5. Joseph Stalin was born in Georgia.

1. When was the Kobe earthquake?

Now continue the quiz with Pair B. Ask and answer each other's questions.

3 *Lesson 1*

Grammar, activity 3

Write five statements about your past, three true and two false.

I was born in Belgium. I married Hercule Poirot.

Now work in pairs. Show your statements to your partner. Your partner must try to guess which are the false statements.

You didn't marry Hercule Poirot!

Now turn back to page 3.

4 *Lesson 1*

Vocabulary and Reading, activity 5

Student A: Ask Student B these questions. Answer his/her questions in turn.

1. Why was Agatha Christie famous?
2. What was the final mystery?
3. When was she born?
4. Where did she live?
5. Who did she marry in 1914?

Now turn back to page 3.

5 *Lesson 16*

Reading and Speaking, activity 3

Student B: You want to know more about the Caribbean Cruise. Ask Student A, who is the travel agent, the following questions and then make a decision:

Will there be a guided tour on Curaçao?
Will we be able to visit both Trinidad and Tobago?
Will there be two twin beds or one queen size bed in the double suites on *The Seaworthy?*

With Student C, decide what to do.

6 *Lesson 8*

Functions and Grammar, activity 3

Student A: Listen to Student B and say what he/she *should/shouldn't* do.

Now act out these situations with Student B. Listen to his/her advice.

– you feel sick
– you feel unhappy all the time
– you are hungry
– you don't like your job

Now turn back to page 18.

7 *Lesson 3*

Vocabulary and Listening, activity 1

Look at the picture for different items of clothing and check that you know what the words mean.

Now turn back to page 6.

8 *Lesson 1*

Vocabulary and Reading, activity 5

Student B: Ask Student A these questions. Answer his/her questions in turn.

1. When did she write her first story?
2. What did she do in December 1926?
3. What did everyone think?
4. Where did her husband find her?
5. Who did she marry in 1930?

Now turn back to page 3.

9 *Lesson 8*

Functions and Grammar, activity 3

Student B: Act out these situations with Student A and listen to his/her advice.

– you don't get enough exercise

– you feel tired all the time

– you are thirsty

– you have a headache

Now listen to Student A and say what he/she *should/shouldn't* do.

Now turn back to page 18.

10 *Lesson 16*

Reading and Speaking, activity 3

Student A: You're a travel agent. Student B and C want to know more about the Caribbean Cruise. Read the information below and answer their questions.

All flights are economy class or business class, but business class is extra.
There will be a personal guided tour on Curaçao or a large-group tour.
They will be able to visit *either* Trinidad *or* Tobago.
There will be two twin beds *or* one queen size bed in the double suites on *The Seaworthy*.
They will stay in a hotel on Trinidad (extra) or on *The Seaworthy* on days 6 and 7.
They will be able to explore Barbados *or* have a scuba diving lesson.

Ask them to make a decision.

11 *Lesson 20*

Reading and Listening, activity 8. Part 4

Going Home

It was the last day of the course at the Modern Language Institute and Jan was very sad. He said goodbye to Mario and his other friends and left the school. That night, Jan and Ruth went for a long walk in the park.

"I love you, Ruth," Jan said.

"I love you too, Jan."

"I'm going home tomorrow. But why don't you come to Poland at Christmas?" said Jan.

"Yes," said Ruth. "I'd love to."

Jan suddenly laughed. "I'm going to see you again!"

Ruth got home at eleven o'clock that evening. She went into the house and her mother met her in the hall.

"You have a visitor, Ruth," she said.

Ruth went into the living room. Bill was there.

The next morning, Ruth went to the airport with Jan.

Jan said, "It's September now. And you're coming to Poland in December."

"I know," said Ruth. "But I'll miss you."

At that moment, they called Jan's flight.

"Goodbye, Ruth," said Jan. "I love you."

"Goodbye, Jan. Write to me."

"Yes, of course."

Ruth drove away from the airport. She went to the park and thought about Jan.

Now turn back to page 47.

12 *Lesson 16*

Reading and Speaking, activity 3

Student C: You want to know more about the Caribbean Cruise. Ask Student A, who is the travel agent, the following questions and then make a decision:

Will the flight from Miami be business class or economy class?

Where will we stay on days 6 and 7?

Will we be able to explore and have a scuba diving lesson on Barbados?

With Student B, decide what to do.

13 *Lesson 2*

Speaking, activity 2

Pair B: Rewrite these facts as quiz questions.

1. The Mexico City earthquake was in 1984.
2. Yuri Gagarin was the first man in space.
3. The first American walked on the moon in 1969.
4. King Henry VIII of England and Wales had six wives.
5. Sigmund Freud was born in Vienna.

1. When was the Mexico City earthquake?

Now continue the quiz with Pair A. Ask and answer each other's questions.

14 *Lesson 10*

Vocabulary and Listening, activity 1

Look at the pictures of different sports and check you know what they are.

15 *Lesson 3*

Reading and Speaking, activity 3

Add up your scores using the following table. Then look at the profiles below to find out what your clothes say about you.

1. a. 2	b. 3	c. 1		**6.** a. 3	b. 2	c. 1
2. a. 2	b. 3	c. 1		**7.** a. 3	b. 2	c. 1
3. a. 2	b. 1	c. 3		**8.** a. 2	b. 1	c. 3
4. a. 2	b. 1	c. 3		**9.** a. 1	b. 3	c. 2
5. a. 3	b. 2	c. 1		**10.** a. 1	b. 2	c. 3

21–30 points. You like to wear exactly what you want. Sometimes this may get you into trouble.

11–20 points. You are quite casual. Sometimes you don't wear the right clothes for the situation.

1–10 points. You're very careful to wear the right clothes for the right situation.

16 *Lesson 20*

Reading and Listening, activity 9. Part 5

The End

Jan wrote several letters to Ruth. But every time Mrs. Clark found the letters she burned them. Ruth was very sad. She thought, Jan doesn't love me any more. He's forgotten about me.

Bill was very kind to Ruth at this time. At the end of November, Ruth went to a party with Bill.

Now turn back to page 47.

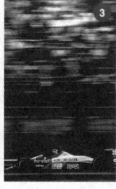

Grammar Review

CONTENTS

Present simple

Form

You use the contracted form in spoken and informal written English.

Be

Affirmative	Negative
I'm (I am)	I'm not (am not)
you	you
we 're (are)	we aren't (are not)
they	they
he	he
she 's (is)	she isn't (is not)
it	it

Questions	Short answers
Am I?	Yes, I am.
	No, I'm not.
Are you/we/they?	Yes, you/we/they are.
	No, you/we/they're not.
Is he/she/it?	Yes, he/she/it is.
	No, he/she/it isn't.

Have

Affirmative	Negative
I	I
you have	you haven't (have not)
we	we
they	they
he	he
she has	she hasn't (has not)
it	it

Questions	Short answers
Have I/you/we/they?	Yes, I/you/we/they have.
	No, I/you/we/they haven't.
Has he/she/it?	Yes, he/she/it has.
	No, he/she/it hasn't.

Regular verbs

Affirmative		Negative	
I		I	
you	work	you	don't (do not) work
we		we	
they		they	
he		he	
she	works	she	doesn't (does not) work
it		it	

Questions	Short answers
Do I/you/we/they work?	Yes, I/you/we/they do.
	No, I/you/we/they don't (do not).
Does he/she/it work?	Yes, he/she/it does.
	No, he/she/it doesn't (does not).

Question words with *is/are*
What's your name?   Where are your parents?

Question words with *does/do*
Where does he live?   What do you do?

Present simple: third person singular

You add *-s* to most verbs.
takes, gets

You add *-es* to *do, go* and verbs which end in
-ch, -ss, -sh, and *-x.*
does, goes, watches, finishes, fixes

You drop the *-y* and add *-ies* to verbs ending in *-y.*
carries, tries

Use
You use the present simple:

to talk about customs. (See Book A, Lesson 7.)
*In Mexico people have dinner at ten or eleven in
the evening.*
*In the United States people leave work at five in the
afternoon.*

to talk about habits and routines. (See Book A, Lesson 9.)
I go running every day.
We see friends on the weekend.

to say how often you do things. (See Book A, Lesson 11.)
I always get up at seven o'clock.
I sometimes go shopping in the evening.

to describe something that is true for a long time.
(See Book B, Lesson 3.)
He wears glasses.

Present continuous

Form

You form the present continuous with *be* + present participle
(*-ing*). You use the contracted form in spoken and informal
written English.

Affirmative		Negative	
I'm (am) working		I'm not (am not) working	
you		you	
we	're (are) working	we	aren't (are not) working
they		they	
he		he	
she	's (is) working	she	isn't (is not) working
it		it	

Questions	Short answers
Am I working?	Yes, I am.
	No, I'm not.
Are you/we/they working?	Yes, you/we/they are.
	No, you/we/they aren't.
Is he/she/it working?	Yes, he/she/it is.
	No, he/she/it isn't.

Question words
What are you doing?   Why are you laughing?

Present participle (*-ing*) endings

You form the present participle of most verbs by adding *-ing*:
go – going   visit – visiting

You drop the final *-e* and add *-ing* to verbs ending in *-e.*
make – making   have – having

You double the final consonant of verbs of one syllable
ending in a single vowel and a consonant and add *-ing.*
get – getting   shop – shopping

You add *-ing* to verbs ending in a vowel and *-y* or *-w.*
draw – drawing   play – playing

You don't usually use these verbs in the continuous form.
*believe feel hate hear know like love see smell
sound taste think understand want*

Use
You use the present continuous:

- to describe something that is happening now or around
  now. (See Book A, Lesson 15 and Book B, Lesson 3.)
  We're flying at 30,000 feet.
  She's wearing a yellow dress.

Past simple

Form

You use the contracted form in spoken and informal written English.

Be

Affirmative	Negative
I	I
he was	he wasn't (was not)
she	she
it	it
you	you
we were	we weren't (were not)
they	they

Have

Affirmative	Negative
I	I
you	you
we	we
they had	they didn't (did not) have
he	he
she	she
it	it

Regular verbs

Affirmative	Negative
I	I
you	you
we	we
they worked	they didn't (did not) work
he	he
she	she
it	it

Questions	Short answers
Did I/you/we/they work?	Yes, I/you/we/they did.
he/she/it	he/she/it
	No, I/you/we/they didn't.
	he/she/it

Question words

What did you do yesterday?   *Why did you leave?*

Past simple endings

You add *-ed* to most regular verbs.
walk – walked   watch – watched

You add *-d* to verbs ending in *-e.*
close – closed   continue – continued

You double the consonant and add *-ed* to verbs of one syllable ending in a single vowel and a consonant.
stop – stopped   plan – planned

You drop the *-y* and add *-ied* to verbs ending in *-y.*
study – studied   try – tried

You add *-ed* to verbs ending in a vowel + *-y.*
play – played   annoy – annoyed

Pronunciation of past simple endings

/t/ *finished, liked, walked*
/d/ *continued, lived, stayed*
/ɪd/ *decided, started, visited*

Expressions of past time
(See Book B, Lesson 2.)

yesterday morning/afternoon/evening
last Saturday/week/month/year
two weeks ago/six months ago

Use

You use the past simple:

● to talk about an action or event in the past that is finished
  (See Book A, Lessons 16, 18, and 20, and Book B, Lesson
  What were you like as a child?
  I started learning English last year.
  Did they go to Hong Kong last year?

Future simple (*will*)

Form

You form the future simple with *will* + infinitive. You use th
contracted form in spoken and informal written English.

Affirmative	Negative
I	I
you	you
we	we
they 'll (will) work	they won't (will not) work
he	he
she	she
it	it

Questions	Short answers
Will I/you/we/they work?	Yes, I/you/we/they will.
he/she/it/	he/she/it/
	No, I/you/we/they won't.
	he/she/it/

Question words

What will you do?   *Where will you go?*

SALLY Yeah? OK, so that's, c.

FRANK Number three, Sony computers are made in Japan, the U.S.A., or Germany?

SALLY Japan.

FRANK Mm… a, then.

SALLY OK, umm, number four. Tea is grown in a, India, b, France, or c, England?

FRANK I think it has to be India, right? Don't you think?

SALLY Yeah, definitely, so that's, a for that one.

FRANK OK, number five, tobacco, where's tobacco grown then, Norway, Iceland, or the U.S.A.? Well it's too cold for Iceland.

SALLY Yeah, it's the U.S.A.

FRANK The U.S.A., that's right, so it's c.

SALLY OK, Benetton clothes are made in Italy, France, or Malaysia?

FRANK Benetton, I think that's Italy, don't you?

SALLY Yeah, I think it is. Yeah.

SALLY Er, number seven, Roquefort cheese is made in a, Germany, b, Thailand, or c, France? It's not Germany, is it?

FRANK No, I don't think it's Germany, I think Roquefort is France.

SALLY Yeah, France, OK.

FRANK Right, number eight. The atom bomb was invented by the Japanese, the Americans, or the Chinese?

SALLY The Americans.

FRANK Yeah, the Americans, b.

SALLY Ah, Guernica was painted by Picasso, Turner, or Monet?

FRANK I have absolutely no idea!

SALLY It's by Picasso, I think.

FRANK Picasso, huh? So that's a.

SALLY Right, the Caribbean islands were discovered by Neil Armstrong, Christopher Columbus, or Marco Polo?

FRANK I think that's Christopher Columbus.

SALLY Was it? Are you sure it wasn't Neil Armstrong?

FRANK Yeah, pretty sure.

SALLY OK, that's b.

FRANK OK, telephone, who invented the telephone, Bell, Marconi, or Baird? Baird invented the television, I think.

SALLY Oh, it's Bell.

FRANK Bell?

SALLY Yeah, definitely.

FRANK OK, twelve, *Romeo and Juliet*, who wrote *Romeo and Juliet*? That's simple, isn't it?

SALLY Yeah.

FRANK Go on, then.

SALLY Well, it wasn't Ibsen.

FRANK No, it has to be Shakespeare.

SALLY Yeah, and it wasn't Stephen King!

FRANK No, that's, b, OK.

SALLY Number thirteen. The Blue Mosque in Istanbul was built for Sultan Ahmet, b, Ataturk, or c, Suleyman the Magnificent?

FRANK Jeez, I have no idea!

SALLY Me, either. Make a guess!

FRANK OK, I'll say it was Ataturk.

SALLY OK, that's, b then.

FRANK *Yesterday*, right who composed *Yesterday*, Paul McCartney, John Lennon, well, it definitely wasn't Mick Jagger.

SALLY No.

FRANK So Paul McCartney or John Lennon? I think I know.

SALLY I think it's, a, Paul McCartney.

FRANK Mm. I think so, too. And finally, the pyramids, who were they built by, the Pharaohs, the Sultans, or Walt Disney?

SALLY Well, not Walt Disney!

FRANK No, I don't think so!

SALLY It was the Pharaohs wasn't it? Yeah, that's, a.

Lesson 19 Listening and Reading, activity 2

CHRIS Good afternoon.

RECEPTIONIST Hi there! Can I help you?

CHRIS Do you have any beds for tonight?

RECEPTIONIST Yes, I think so. You see, I just started work at the hostel. How long would you like to stay?

CHRIS We'll stay for just one night.

RECEPTIONIST Yes, that's OK.

TONY Great!

RECEPTIONIST How old are you?

TONY We're both sixteen.

RECEPTIONIST OK, that'll be $13 each.

CHRIS Is it far from the hostel to Eureka?

RECEPTIONIST No, not really, it's two miles. It takes about an hour on foot.

TONY Is there a bus?

RECEPTIONIST I think so. It takes about fifteen minutes. There's a bus every hour.

TONY What time is the last bus from Eureka?

RECEPTIONIST I think it leaves at nine o'clock. There's not much to do at night.

CHRIS We're exhausted! We need to go to bed early. What time does the hostel close in the morning?

RECEPTIONIST Umm, at eleven A.M. Where are you walking to?

CHRIS We're going to Crescent City. Are you serving dinner tonight?

RECEPTIONIST Yes, we're serving dinner until eight o'clock. And breakfast starts at seven thirty.

TONY And where's the nearest campsite?

RECEPTIONIST I'm not sure. I think it's Fortuna, which is about ten miles north of here. I started work last Monday so I'm very new here.

Lesson 19 Listening and Reading, activity 4

CHRIS It's very strange. She said one night cost $13, but it costs $12.

TONY Yes, and she said it was two miles to Eureka.

CHRIS But, in fact, it's three miles.

TONY And she said the last bus left at nine o'clock. But it leaves at eight o'clock.

Lesson 19 Grammar, activity 3

CHRIS And she said the bus took fifteen minutes. But in fact, it takes ten minutes.

TONY And she said the hostel closed at eleven A.M., but it's open all day.

CHRIS The brochure says that they serve dinner from six to seven.

TONY But she said they were serving until eight o'clock. And she also said breakfast started at seven thirty…

CHRIS … when, in fact, it says here that breakfast starts at seven.

TONY And she said that Fortuna was ten miles away, but it isn't. It's eight miles away.

CHRIS And she said that Fortuna was north of here. But it's south of here!

Lesson 20 Reading and Listening, activity 6

Ruth's Parents

The next afternoon, Jan went over to Ruth's house for tea.

"How do you do, Mr. and Mrs. Clark," Jan said.

"Sit down, Jan," said Mrs. Clark. "Would you like a cup of coffee?"

"Yes, please," said Jan. He didn't feel very comfortable.

Jan stayed for about an hour. Mr. Clark spoke English very quickly and Jan did not always understand.

Outside the door, Jan said to Ruth, "Your parents don't like me very much."

"Don't be silly, Jan," said Ruth. "My parents haven't met many foreigners. It's all right."

"OK, Ruth," said Jan. "I'll see you tomorrow." And he walked away. But he felt unhappy.

Later that evening Ruth asked, "Well, Mom, did you like Jan?"

Ruth's mother said, "Well, he didn't speak English very well. Your father and I liked Bill. What's wrong with an American boyfriend? And Jan is going back to Poland soon."

"But I don't like Bill any more," shouted Ruth and ran out of the room. "I don't like Bill," she said to herself, "but I do like Jan. Maybe I love him."

Wordlist

The first number after each word shows the lesson in which the word first appears in the vocabulary box. The numbers in *italics* show the later lessons in which the word appears again

adult /ˈædʌlt/ 19
anniversary /ˌæniˈvɜːsəri/ 13
apple pie /ˈæpe(ə)l paɪ/ 5
April /ˈeɪprɪl/ 2
area /ˈeərɪə/ 9
arm /ɑːm/ 8
arrival hall /əˈraɪv(ə)l hɔːl/ 16
aspirin /ˈæsprɪn/ 8
August /ˈɔːgəst/ 2
average /ˈævərɪdʒ/ 9

back /bæk/ 8
badly /ˈbædlɪ/ 15
baggage reclaim
  /ˈbægɪdʒ rɪˈkleɪm/ 16
bar /bɑː(r)/ 6
barbecue /ˈbɑːbɪˌkjuː/ 14
baseball /ˈbeɪsbɔːl/ 10
basketball /ˈbɑːskɪtˌbɔːl/ 10
big /bɪg/ 9
blanket /ˈblæŋkɪt/ 14
boarding pass /bɔːdɪŋ pɑːs/ 16
bottle /ˈbɒt(ə)l/ 6
bottle opener
  /ˈbɒt(ə)l ˈəʊpənə(r)/ 14
box /bɒks/ 6
boyfriend /ˈbɔɪfrend/ 20
bridge /brɪdʒ/ 12
build /ˈbɪld/ 18
bunch /bʌntʃ/ 6
business class
  /ˈbɪznɪs klɒːs/ 16

cakes /keɪkz/ 6
camp site /kæmp saɪt/ 19
carefully /ˈkeəfʊlɪ/ 15
carelessly /ˈkeəlɪslɪ/ 15
carton /ˈkɑːt(ə)n/ 14
cash /kæʃ/ 13
casual /ˈkæʒʊəl/ 3
celebrate /ˈseləbreɪt/ 13
change /tʃeɪndʒ/ 4
charges /ˈtʃɑːdʒɪz/ 19
check-in /ˈtʃek ɪn/ 16
cheeseburger /ˈtʃiːsbɜːgə/ 5
cheesecake /ˈtʃiːzkeɪk/ 5

chocolate /ˈtʃɒkələt/ 6
climb /klaɪm/ 12
climbing /klaɪmɪŋ/ 10
cloud /klaʊd/ 17
coffee /ˈkɒfɪ/ 5
coffee shop /ˈkɒfɪ ʃɒp/ 20
coke /kəʊk/ 5
cold /kəʊld/ 9, 17
cold (*noun*) /kəʊld/ 8
comfortable /ˈkʌmftəb(ə)l/ 3
compose /kɒmˈpəʊs/ 18
cookies /ˈkʊkiːs/ 6
cool /kuːl/ 17
cooler /kuːlə/ 14
cough /kɒf/ 8
cough medicine
  /kɒf ˈmedsɪn/ 8
cover /ˈkʌvə(r)/ 11
crime /kraɪm/ 13
cruise /kruːz/ 16
cup /kʌp/ 14
cycling /ˈsaɪklɪŋ/ 10

dangerous /ˈdeɪndʒərəs/ 10
December /dɪˈsembə(r)/ 2
deli /deli/ 13
departure gate
  /dɪˈpɑːtʃə(r) geɪt/ 16
departure lounge
  /dɪˈpɑːtʃə(r) laʊndʒ/ 16
detective story
  /dɪˈtektɪv ˈstɔːrɪ/ 1
difficult /ˈdɪfɪkəlt/ 10
director /daɪˈrektə(r)/ 20
disappear /ˌdɪsəˈpɪə(r)/ 1
disco /ˈdɪskəʊ/ 13
discover /dɪsˈkʌvə/ 18
divorced /dɪˈvɔːsd/ 1
dizzy /ˈdɪzɪ/ 8
dress /dres/ 3
dry /draɪ/ 9, 17

economy class /ɪˈkɒnəmɪ klɑːs/
  16
education /edʒʊˈkeɪʃən/ 9
eighth /eɪtθ/ 2
eleventh /ɪˈlevənθ/ 2
exciting /ɪkˈsaɪtɪŋ/ 10
expensive /ɪkˈspensɪv/ 10

facilities /fəˈsɪlɪtɪz/ 19
Fahrenheit /ˈfærənhaɪt/ 9
faint /feɪnt/ 8
fashionable /ˈfæʃnəb(ə)l/ 3, 10
fast /fɑːst/ 9

February /ˈfebrʊərɪ/ 2
fifth /fɪfθ/ 2
find /faɪnd/ 1
finger /ˈfɪŋgə(r)/ 8
first /fɜːst/ 2
first class /fɜːst klɑːs/ 16
flowers /ˈflaʊə(r)z/ 6
fog /fɒg/ 17
foggy /ˈfɒgɪ/ 17
foot /fʊt/ 8, 9
football /ˈfʊtbɔːl/ 10
foreigner /ˈfɒrɪnə(r)/ 20
forget /fəˈget/ 20
fork /fɔːk/ 14
formal /ˈfɔːməl/ 3
fourth /fɔːθ/ 2
French fries /frentʃ fraɪz/ 5

get /get/ 4
glass /glɑːs/ 7
golden /ˈgəʊldən/ 13
golf /gɒlf/ 10
grow /grəʊ/ 18
guest /gest/ 1

hand /hænd/ 8
hang gliding /ˈhæŋglaɪdɪŋ/ 10
headache /ˈhedeɪk/ 8
heavy /ˈhevɪ/ 7
high /haɪ/ 9
hill /hɪl/ 12
horseriding /ˈhɔːsraɪdɪŋ/ 10
hot /hɒt/ 9, 17
hot dog /hɒt dɒg/ 5
hot tub /hɒt tʊb/ 19
hotel /həʊˈtel/ 1
husband /ˈhʌzbənd/ 1

ice cream /aɪs kriːm/ 5
immigrant /ˈɪmɪgrənt/ 13
inch /ɪntʃ/ 9
invent /ɪnˈvent/ 18
invite /ɪnˈvaɪt/ 4

jacket /ˈdʒækɪt/ 3
January /ˈdʒænjʊərɪ/ 2
jeans /dʒiːnz/ 3, 6
jello /ˈdʒeləʊ/ 5
juice /dʒuːs/ 5
July /dʒuːˈlaɪ/ 2
June /dʒuːn/ 2

kill /kɪl/ 1
kiss /kɪs/ 11
knife /naɪf/ 14

language school
  /ˈlæŋgwɪdʒ skuːl/ 20
large /lɑːdʒ/ 7
laugh /lɑːf/ 3
leather /ˈleðə(r)/ 7
left home /left həʊm/ 1
leg /leg/ 8
light /laɪt/ 7
long /lɒŋ/ 7
loudly /ˈlaʊdlɪ/ 15
love /lʌv/ 20
low /ləʊ/ 9

make /meɪk/ 18
March /mɑːtʃ/ 2
marriage /ˈmærɪdʒ/ 1
matches /mætʃɪz/ 14
May /meɪ/ 2
mayonnaise /ˌmeɪəˈneɪz/ 5
metal /ˈmet(ə)l/ 7
mile /maɪl/ 9
milk /mɪlk/ 6
miss /mɪs/ 20
motor racing
  /ˈməʊtə(r) reɪsɪŋ/ 10
mystery /ˈmɪstərɪ/ 1

neighborhood /ˈneɪbəhʊd/
ninth /naɪnθ/ 1
no smoking /nəʊ ˈsməʊkɪŋ/
November /nəˈvenbə(r)/ 2

October /ɒkˈtəʊbə(r)/ 2
old /əʊld/ 9
on board /ɒn bɔːd/ 16
one-way /wʌn weɪ/ 16
outdoor /aʊtdɔː/ 19

package /pækɪdʒ/ 6
paint /peɪnt/ 18
pair /peə(r)/ 6
pants /pænts/ 3
paper /ˈpeɪpə(r)/ 7
park /pɑːk/ 12
passport control
  /ˈpɑːspɔːt kənˈtrəʊl/ 16
perfume /ˈpɜːfjuːm/ 6
pizza /ˈpiːtsə/ 5
plastic /ˈplæstɪk/ 7
point at /ˈpɔɪnt æt/ 11
politely /pəˈlaɪtlɪ/ 15
popular /ˈpɒpjʊlə(r)/ 10
population /pɒpjʊleɪʃən/ 9
port /pɔːt/ 16

66

quickly /ˈkwɪklɪ/ 15
quietly /ˈkwaɪətlɪ/ 15

rain /reɪn/ 17
rainfall /ˈreɪnfɔːl/ 9
rainy /ˈreɪnɪ/ 17
rectangular /rekˈtæŋɡʊlə(r)/ 7
retire /rəˈtaɪə(r)/ 13
rob /rɒb/ 13
round /raʊnd/ 7
round-trip /raʊnd trɪp/ 16
rudely /ˈruːdlɪ/ 15

salad /ˈsæləd/ 5
sandwich /ˈsænwɪdʒ/ 5
save /seɪv/ 4
second /ˈsekənd/ 2
September /sepˈtembə(r)/ 2
seventh /ˈsev(ə)nθ/ 2
shake hands /ʃeɪk hænds/ 11
shirt /ʃɜːt/ 3
shoes /ʃuːs/ 3
short /ʃɔːt/ 7
shorts /ʃɔːtz/ 3
sick /sɪk/ 8
sight /saɪt/ 13
sit down /sɪt daʊn/ 3
sixth /sɪksθ/ 1
skiing /skiːɪŋ/ 10
skirt /skɜːt/ 3
slow /sləʊ/ 9
slowly /sləʊlɪ/ 15
small /smɔːl/ 7, 9
smile /smaɪl/ 3
sneakers /ˈsniːkəs/ 3
snow /snəʊ/ 17
snowy /snəʊɪ/ 17
soap /səʊp/ 6
soccer /sɒkə/ 10
socks /sɒks/ 3
sore throat /sɔː(r) θrəʊt/ 8
spaghetti /spəˈɡetɪ/ 5
spend /spend/ 4
square /skweə(r)/ 7
square mile /skweə(r) maɪl/ 9
stand /stænd/ 3
steak /steɪk/ 5
step /step/ 20
stomach ache /ˈstʌmək eɪk/ 8
strange /streɪndʒ/ 20
strawberry /ˈstrɔːbərɪ/ 5
subway /sʌbweɪ/ 13
successful /səkˈsesfʊl/ 1
sun /sʌn/ 17
sunny /sʌnɪ/ 17
sweater /ˈswetə(r)/ 3
swimming /swɪmɪŋ/ 10

T-shirt /tiː ˈʃɜːt/ 3
take /teɪk/ 4
take off /taɪk ɒf/ 11
tell /tel/ 1
temperature /ˈtemprɪtʃə(r)/ 8, 9
tenth /tenθ/ 2
third /θɜːd/ 2
tie /taɪ/ 3
tired /ˈtaɪəd/ 8
tiring /ˈtaɪərɪŋ/ 10
toe /təʊ/ 8
trash /træʃ/ 14
travel /ˈtrævəl/ 19
travel agency /trævəl eɪdʒənsɪ/ 16
twelfth /twelfθ/ 2

unhappy /ʌnˈhæpɪ/ 1

view /vjuː/ 12
visitor /ˈvɪzɪtə/ 20

waiter /ˈweɪtə(r)/ 1
war /wɔː/ 13
warm /wɔːm/ 3, 17
wear /weə(r)/ 3
well /wel/ 15
wet /wet/ 9, 17
wind /wɪnd/ 17
windsurfing /ˈwɪndˌsɜːfɪŋ/ 10
windy /ˈwɪndɪ/ 17
wood /wʊd/ 7
write /raɪt/ 18
writer /ˈraɪtə(r)/ 1

yard /jɑːd/ 9
young /jʌŋ/ 9
youth hostel /juː ˈhɒst(ə)l/ 19

Lesson 18 Reading and Writing, activity 4

A: coffee
B: tobacco

67

Progress Test 1 Lessons 1–10

SECTION 1: VOCABULARY (30 points)

1. a. Underline the word which doesn't belong and leave a group of three related words. (10 points)

b. Add one other word to the groups of words. (10 points)

Example: her my our <u>they</u> *their*

1. eight first ninth third _____

2. August March Monday July _____

3. casual socks sweater tie _____

4. coffee salad pizza steak _____

5. black light round short _____

6. bag glass paper plastic _____

7. his mine whose yours _____

8. cough headache medicine temperature

_____

9. best biggest fast worst _____

10. basketball cycling knitting skiing _____

2. Complete these sentences with ten different verbs. (10 points)

Example: I __*work*__ in an office.

1. I _____ stories in my free time.

2. I _____ to the dentist twice a year.

3. I _____ comfortable clothes.

4. I _____ a lot of exercise.

5. I _____ eight hours a day at work.

6. I _____ hands when I meet people.

7. I _____ gifts for my friends on their birthdays.

8. I _____ sick.

9. I _____ plenty of water.

10. I _____ hang gliding is dangerous.

Progress Test 1 Lessons 1–10

SECTION 2: GRAMMAR (30 points)

3. a. Choose ten of these words to complete the first ten spaces in the conversation. (10 points)

Example: a) Are b) Do c) <u>Would</u>

1. a) I'm not b) I don't c) I wouldn't
2. a) a b) any c) some
3. a) they b) we c) you
4. a) How b) Why c) What
5. a) me b) mine c) my
6. a) did b) do c) will
7. a) in b) next c) on
8. a) two b) to c) too
9. a) from b) of c) with
10. a) because b) but c) so

b. Complete the last ten spaces with ten of your own words. (10 points)

CHRIS: <u>Would</u> you like a cup of coffee?

JANE: No, thank you. (1) _____ like coffee. Can I have (2) _____ water?

CHRIS: Yes, here (3) _____ are.

JANE: (4) _____ was your skiing trip?

CHRIS: Great, but I lost (5) _____ ski jacket.

JANE: Where (6) _____ you lose it?

CHRIS: I don't know. It was on my bag and maybe I left it (7) _____ a chair at the airport.

JANE: That's (8) _____ bad! It was a nice jacket.

CHRIS: Yes, it was. It was very light.

JANE: What was it made (9) _____?

CHRIS: Gortex. I bought it (10) _____ it was light.

CLERK: Good afternoon. (11) _____ I help you?

CHRIS: Yes, I'm looking (12) _____ a ski jacket.

CLERK: We've got some ski jackets (13) _____ there.

CHRIS: This purple one is nice. Can I try it (14) _____?

CLERK: Yes, go (15) _____.

CHRIS: No, it doesn't fit (16) _____. Do you have one in a bigger size?

CLERK: No, I'm afraid (17) _____. That's the (18) _____ one in that color.

CHRIS: Do you have it (19) _____ green?

CLERK: Not in a larger size. What about the black one?

CHRIS: No, black doesn't look good on me. I'll leave (20) _____. Thank you.

4. Write these sentences in the negative. (10 points)

Example: I can speak French.
I can't speak French.

1. She has an aspirin.

   _____

2. He found his coat.

   _____

3. They had a happy marriage.

   _____

4. We like horseback riding.

   _____

5. I'm older than John.

   _____

6. He's wearing brown shoes.

   _____

7. You should sit down.

   _____

8. She does the housework.

   _____

9. It was wet.

   _____

10. We're going away this year.

   _____

Progress Test 1 Lessons 1–10

SECTION 3: READING (20 points)

5. Read the passage *The Olympic Games*.
Are these sentences true (T) or false (F) or doesn't
the passage say (DS)? (10 points)

Example: The ancient games took place in different
cities. [F]

1. Women took part in the first modern

   Olympic games. □

2. The ancient games included ball games. □

3. There were no games for about 1,500 years. □

4. Norma Enriqueta Basilio de Sotela won a medal. □

5. Mark Spitz swam in more than one Olympic

   games. □

6. Answer the questions. (10 points)

Example: Where were the first Olympic games?
They were in Olympia, in Greece.

1. What happened for the first time in 1968?

   _____

2. How many teams were at the Atlanta games?

   _____

3. Why are there five rings in the Olympic symbol?

   _____

4. What happened about a hundred years ago?

   _____

5. In which year did beach volleyball first become an

   Olympic sport?

   _____

THE OLYMPIC GAMES

* The Olympic Games began in Greece more
than 2,000 years ago. Young men from
different cities took part in running,
horseback riding, boxing, and riding. No
women took part in or watched the games.

* The last ancient games took place in the year
394 and for many hundreds of years there
were no games. Then, in 1896 the first modern
Olympic Games took place, again in Greece.
Most countries send a team of athletes to the
games. In the 1996 games, 197 countries sent
teams to Atlanta. Beach volleyball became an
Olympic sport for the first time.

* At the start of the Olympic Games, an athlete
runs into the Olympic stadium with a torch
and lights an Olympic flame. The flame comes
all the way from Olympia. The lighting of the
torch is part of an enormous opening
ceremony. In 1968 Mexican hurdler,
Norma Enriqueta Basilio de Sotela, became
the first woman to light the Olympic flame.

* The Olympic symbol is five colored rings.
These rings represent the five continents in
the world.

* Winners receive gold, silver, or bronze
medals. Sometimes competitors win more
than one medal. In 1972, Mark Spitz, an
American swimmer, won seven gold medals.
He also broke four world records.

Progress Test 1 Lessons 1–10

SECTION 4: WRITING (20 points)

7. Write a short autobiography. Write about some special events in your life. Write 8 – 10 sentences. (20 points)

_____

_____

_____

_____

_____

_____

_____

_____

_____

_____

_____

_____

_____

_____

_____

_____

_____

_____

_____

_____

Progress Test 2 Lessons 11–20

SECTION 1: VOCABULARY (30 points)

1. a. Write two words from the box in each category below. (10 points)

> aunt drugstore chair China cough cupboard
>
> cycling December ferry flower shop golf
>
> headache Hungary journalist March plane
>
> salad sister sweater tie waiter water

Example:

clothes	*sweater*	*tie*
medical conditions		
countries		
family		
food and drink		
furniture		
jobs		
means of transportation		
months		
stores		
sports		

b. Add one other word to the categories. (10 points)

clothes	
medical conditions	
countries	
family	
food and drink	
furniture	
jobs	
means of transportation	
months	
stores	
sports	

2. Complete these sentences with ten different verbs. (10 points)

Example: I _have_ lunch at home.

1. I _____ photographs with my camera.

2. I often _____ in hotels when I go on vacation.

3. I _____ to music on my radio.

4. I always _____ my bills every month.

5. I _____ a knife to cut meat.

6. I usually _____ a list before I go shopping.

7. I _____ clearly so everyone can hear me.

8. I don't _____ exams very easily.

9. I _____ hard at school.

10. I sometimes _____ a touchdown when I play football.

Progress Test 2 Lessons 11–20

SECTION 2: GRAMMAR (30 points)

3. a. Choose ten of these words to complete the first ten spaces in the conversation. (10 points)

Example: a) phones b) _phone's_ c) phones'

1. a) I b) I'll c) I'm

2. a) How b) Where c) Who

3. a) right b) exactly c) soon

4. a) not b) so c) very

5. a) ever b) never c) yet

6. a) has been b) is c) was

7. a) ago b) last c) past

8. a) go b) have gone c) went

9. a) are you staying b) do you stay c) have you stayed

10. a) in b) on c) this

b. Complete the last ten spaces with ten of your own words. (10 points)

JAMIE: Chris! The _phone's_ ringing.

CHRIS: OK, (1) _____ answer it. ... Hello, 379-4624.

JANE: Hi, Chris! It's Jane.

CHRIS: Jane! (2) _____ are you?

JANE: I'm fine. I'm in New York with Beth (3) _____ now. We've been here two days but we've done (4) _____ much already. Have you (5) _____ been to New York?

CHRIS: Yes, I have.

JANE: When (6) _____ that?

CHRIS: Three years (7) _____ . I (8) _____ to a conference there. It was great. Where (9) _____ ?

JANE: In a hotel on Fifth Avenue. It's near Central Park. We went there (10) _____ morning. Central Park can be dangerous but we (11) _____ careful.

CHRIS: Have you been to the Statue of Liberty? I've (12) _____ finished reading an article about it. It (13) _____ opened in 1885. (14) _____ you know that?

JANE: No, I didn't. We'll probably go there (15) _____ Monday morning. There's a ferry from Manhattan (16) _____ half hour.

CHRIS: How's Beth? Is she (17) _____ a good time?

JANE: She (18) _____ a cold. I think she (19) _____ take some aspirin, but she won't. She says it'll (20) _____ better tomorrow.

4. Underline the correct expression in the sentences below. (10 points)

Example: I'd like _dancing/to dance_.

1. _I/I've_ moved to Texas when I was eighteen.

2. _I/I'd_ like a ticket to Boston.

3. The Taj Mahal _built/was built_ by Shah Jehan.

4. He said he _is/was_ going to call yesterday.

5. It _takes/is taking_ ten minutes by car.

6. He _doesn't speak/isn't speaking_ English very well.

7. My birthday _has been/was_ in June.

8. I have lived here _for/since_ two years.

9. My back _hurt/hurts_ when I sat down.

10. _I'm wearing/I wear_ trainers today.

Progress Test 2 Lessons 11–20

SECTION 3: READING (20 points)

5. Read the passage *Rice*.
Check the correct answers. (10 points)

Example: People in China

a) are enormous.
b) eat a lot of rice. ✓
c) greet each other with rice.
d) need a lot of water.

1. Most of the world's rice is grown

a) in Australia.
b) in Asia.
c) on hills.
d) in Japan.

2. Asian countries

a) always produce enough rice.
b) don't have any flat land.
c) produce more potatoes than rice.
d) sometimes have to import rice.

3. Rice is planted

a) by machine in Asia.
b) by hand and picked by machine.
c) by hand in the United States.
d) by hand in most Asian countries.

4. North Americans

a) don't like potatoes.
b) eat more bread than rice.
c) don't eat rice.
d) prefer rice from China.

5. Rice was grown in Egypt

a) before it was grown in China.
b) after it was grown in Italy.
c) before it was grown in Europe.
d) after it was grown in the U.S.A.

RICE

Rice is one of the most important foods in the world. This is because people who live in China, Japan, India, and other parts of Asia, live mainly on rice. In China the word "rice" is used in one of their greetings. People say "Have you eaten your rice today?" This is because rice is so important to the Chinese.

Although most of the world's rice is produced in Asia, sometimes it has to be imported. This happens when rice doesn't grow properly. If there is no rice harvest, people in Asia may die.

Rice was first grown in China about five thousand years ago and it was then introduced into Egypt.

Rice was first grown in Europe, in Italy, about six hundred years ago. It was not grown until three hundred years ago in the United States. North Americans eat some rice but they prefer bread and potatoes.

Some rice is grown on hills but most rice is grown on flat land near lakes and rivers, because rice needs a lot of water. In the rice-growing parts of the United States, rice is planted and picked by machine, but in most Asian countries everything is done by hand.

6. Are these sentences true (T) or false (F), or doesn't the passage say (DS)? (10 points)

Example: All Asian people eat 400–800 kilograms of rice a year. ☐F

1. North Americans eat more rice than Europeans. ☐

2. Rice is grown near lakes and rivers because it needs a lot of water. ☐

3. Rice was probably grown in Egypt more than five thousand years ago. ☐

4. North Americans have just started eating rice. ☐

5. Machines are never used to plant or pick rice in Asia. ☐

Progress Test 2 Lessons 11–20

SECTION 4: WRITING (20 points)

7. Write about one day last week. Write about something special or unusual you did. Write 8 – 10 sentences. (20 points)

_____

_____

_____

_____

_____

_____

_____

_____

_____

_____

_____

_____

_____

_____

_____

_____

_____

_____

_____

_____

_____

_____

Answers Progress Test 1 Lessons 1–10

SECTION 1: VOCABULARY [30 points]

1. a. (10 points: 1 point for each correct answer.)

1. eight		6. bag	
2. Monday		7. whose	
3. casual		8. medicine	
4. coffee		9. fast	
5. black		10. knitting	

b. (10 points: 1 point for each appropriate answer.)
1. an ordinal number, e.g. *second, fourth*
2. a month, e.g. *January, May*
3. an item of clothing, e.g. *jeans, T-shirt*
4. something to eat, e.g. *cheesecake, sandwich*
5. an adjective for describing an object, e.g. *heavy, large*
6. a material, e.g. *leather, metal*
7. a possessive pronoun, e.g. *hers, ours*
8. a medical complaint, e.g. *sore throat, stomachache*
9. a superlative adjective, e.g. *dirtiest, oldest*
10. a sport, e.g. *boxing, baseball*

2. (10 points: 1 point for each appropriate answer.)

1. write/read		6. shake	
2. go		7. buy	
3. wear		8. am/feel	
4. do/get		9. drink	
5. spend		10. think	

SECTION 2: GRAMMAR [30 points]

3. a. (10 points: 1 point for each correct answer.)

1. b) I don't		6. a) did	
2. c) some		7. c) on	
3. c) you		8. c) too	
4. a) How		9. b) of	
5. c) my		10. a) because	

b. (10 points: 1 point for each appropriate answer.)
Possible Answers

11. Can/May		16. me	
12. for		17. not	
13. over		18. biggest/only	
14. on		19. in	
15. ahead		20. it	

4. (10 points: 1 point for each correct sentence.)
1. She doesn't have an aspirin.
2. He didn't find his coat.
3. They didn't have a happy marriage.
4. We don't like horseback riding.
5. I'm not older than John.
6. He isn't wearing brown shoes.
7. You shouldn't sit down.
8. She doesn't do the housework.
9. It wasn't wet.
10. We aren't going away this year.

SECTION 3: READING [20 points]

5. (10 points: 2 points for each correct answer.)
1. DS 2. F 3. T 4. DS 5. DS

6. (10 points: 2 points for each correct answer.)
1. (For the first time in 1968) a woman lit the Olympic flame.
2. 197 (teams were at the Atlanta games).
3. (There are five rings) because there are five continents in the world.
4. The first modern Olympic Games took place (about a hundred years ago).
5. (Beach volleyball first became an Olympic sport) in 1996.

SECTION 4: WRITING [20 points]

7. (20 points)
Tell students what you will take into consideration when grading their written work. Criteria should include:
* efficient communication of meaning (7 points)
* grammatical accuracy (7 points)
* coherence in the ordering or the information or ideas (3 points)
* layout, capitalization, and punctuation (3 points)

It is probably better not to use a rigid grading system with the written part of the test. If, for example, you always deduct a point for a grammatical mistake, you may find that you are over-penalizing students who write a lot or who take risks. Deduct points if students haven't written the minimum number of sentences stated in the test.

Answers Progress Test 2 Lessons 11–20

SECTION 1: VOCABULARY [30 points]

1. a. (10 points: 1 point for each correct answer.)

medical conditions	cough, headache
countries	China, Hungary
family	aunt, sister
food and drink	salad, water
furniture	chair, cupboard
jobs	journalist, waiter
means of transportation	ferry, plane
months	December, March
stores	drugstore, flower shop
sports	cycling, golf

b. (10 points: 1 point for each appropriate answer.)

medical conditions	e.g. *cold, stomachache*
countries	e.g. *France, Spain*
family	e.g. *husband, mother*
food and drink	e.g. *bread, French fries*
furniture	e.g. *bed, table*
jobs	e.g. *secretary, teacher*
means of transportation	e.g. *bicycle, train*
months	e.g. *July, September*
stores	e.g. *music store, grocery store*
sports	e.g. *boxing, baseball*

2. (10 points: 1 point for each appropriate answer.)

1. take	6. make
2. stay	7. speak
3. listen	8. pass
4. pay	9. work
5. use	10. score

SECTION 2: GRAMMAR [30 points]

3. a. (10 points: 1 point for each correct answer.)

1. b) I'll	6. c) was
2. a) How	7. a) ago
3. a) right	8. c) went
4. b) so	9. a) are you staying
5. a) ever	10. c) this

b. (10 points: 1 point for each appropriate answer.)
Possible Answers

11. were	16. every
12. just	17. having
13. was	18. has
14. Did	19. should
15. on	20. be

4. (10 points: 1 point for each correct expression.)

1. I	6. doesn't speak
2. I'd	7. was
3. was built	8. for
4. was	9. hurt
5. takes	10. I'm wearing

SECTION 3: READING [20 points]

5. (10 points: 2 points for each correct answer.)
1. b 2. d 3. d 4. b 5. c

6. (10 points: 2 points for each correct answer.)
1. DS 2. T 3. F 4. F 5. F

SECTION 4: WRITING [20 points]

7. (20 points)
Tell students what you will take into consideration when grading their written work. Criteria should include:
* efficient communication of meaning (7 points)
* grammatical accuracy (7 points)
* coherence in the ordering or the information or ideas (3 points)
* layout, capitalization, and punctuation (3 points)

It is probably better not to use a rigid grading system with the written part of the test. If, for example, you always deduct a point for a grammatical mistake, you may find that you are over-penalizing students who write a lot or who take risks. Deduct points if students haven't written the minimum number of sentences stated in the test.

Answer Key

Lesson 1

GRAMMAR AND VOCABULARY
1. encouraged   informed
   <u>thought</u>   <u>sold</u>   married
   <u>left</u>   <u>found</u>   refused
2. 1. c 2. d 3. e 4. g 5. b 6. a 7. f
3. 1. We didn't go to Hawaii on
   vacation.
   2. She didn't write to her
   husband.
   3. She wasn't born in Australia.
   4. The police didn't find her.
   5. They didn't have a nice
   evening.
   6. He wasn't late yesterday.

READING
1. William Shakespeare
   was   was   went   married   had
   left   went   did   lived   worked
   stopped   was   wrote   wrote
   finished   left   went   died
2. 2. When was he born?
   3. Where did he go to school?
   4. Who did he marry?
   5. Where did he work as an
   actor?
   6. When did he stop acting?
   7. Why did he stop acting?
   8. When did he write his first
   play?
   9. Where did he go in 1612?
   10. When did he die?
3. Between 1585 and 1590.
4. 1. He was born in Stratford.
   2. He was born in 1564.
   3. He went to the local grade
   school.
   4. He married Anne Hathaway.
   5. He worked in London.
   6. He stopped acting in 1603.
   7. Because he was famous for his
   writing.
   8. He wrote his first play in
   1590–91.
   9. He went back to Stratford.
   10. He died in 1616.

WRITING
1. was   moved   was   lived
   went   wrote   became
2. *Possible Answer*
   Mark Twain was born in
   Missouri, U.S.A in 1835. We
   know that he worked as a ship's
   pilot on the Mississippi in 1857
   and he became a journalist in
   1862. He went on a tour of
   Europe in 1865 and in 1876 he
   wrote *The Adventures of Tom
   Sawyer*. He died in 1910.

Lesson 2

VOCABULARY AND SOUNDS
1. fifth   sixth   eighth   ninth
   twelfth   thirteenth   fifteenth
2. *Nouns:* discovery,   discoverer
   explosion   invention,   inventor
   landing   painting,   painter
   take-off   win,   winner,   winnings
3. 1. won   2. discovered
   3. exploded   4. painted
   5. invented   6. landed

READING
1. B
2. *Columbia*, the first space shuttle
   took off.
   Challenger exploded after
   take-off.
   NASA put the Hubble Space
   Telescope into space.
   Endeavor replaced *Challenger*.

GRAMMAR
1. in June, in 1995, in the evening,
   in the morning
   on Friday, on the March 26
   on the weekend, at night
   yesterday
   night/evening/morning
   last month/weekend/night
   a month/week ago 10 years ago
5. 1. afternoon   2. two years
   3. 1985   4. 1988   5. year
   6. six months   7. spring

Lesson 3

VOCABULARY
1. *Across:* 1. jacket   4. shorts
   7. shoe   8 skirt   10. blouse
   Down: 1. jeans   2. coat
   3. t-shirt   5. suit   6. boots
   7. sock   9 tie
4. **TO BE CHECKED WITH FINAL
   A/W**
5. A: formal   B: casual
   C: fashionable

READING AND GRAMMAR
1. 1. Pat is writing to Sarah.
   2. Pat is on vacation in New
   Zealand.
   3. She is Pat's mother's cousin.
2. *Present continuous:* I'm having
   I'm staying   she's taking
   I'm staying   I'm staying
   I'm flying
   Present simple: she's
   Aunt Grace is   she's   She has
   she wears   she smiles   she talks
   she is   she reads
   she doesn't know
   she never goes   she says   it's
   she's   we visit   the scenery is
3. expensive – the trip to Canada
   wonderful – her vacation
   beautiful – the scenery
   big – Aunt Grace's eyes
   interesting – Aunt Grace
   happy – Aunt Grace
4. 1. are staying   2. live   3. wears
   4. is looking 5. goes 6. is
   laughing

Lesson 4

VOCABULARY
1. 1. study   2. stop   3. worry
   4. save   5. spend   6. invite
2. 1. d   2. f   3. e   4. b   5. a   6. c

GRAMMAR
1. *Possible Answers*
   1. He's going to fly to Hawaii.
   2. They're going to see a football
   game.
   3. They're going to play tennis.
   4. She's going go the shopping.

READING
1. c: retirement plans
2. 1. sixty-five   2. work   3. trip/
   vacation   4. Central and South
   America   5. move, Manhattan
   6. apartment, park

WRITING
1. magazine fashion writer
2. *Possible Answers*
   On Monday she's going to visit
   the hat exhibition at the new art
   and design college at 2 P.M.
   On Tuesday at 7:15 A.M. she's
   going to fly to Los Angeles. At
   1 P.M. she's going to do an
   interview with a Los Angeles
   clothes designer.
   On Wednesday she's going to an
   editorial meeting for the January
   edition of the magazine.
   On Thursday she's going to the
   New York spring clothes
   preview.
   On Friday she's going to finish
   her article on hats.
   On Saturday she's going to Pete
   and Jenny's party.
   On Sunday she's going to visit
   her parents in Connecticut.

Lesson 5

VOCABULARY
1. a. waiter   b. check   c. tip
   d. starter   e. coffee
   f. reservation   g. menu
   h. course, dessert   i. taste
   j. order
2. 1. f   2. a   3. g   4. j   5. i   6. d
   7. h   8. e   9. b   10. c

READING
1. in a bar   2. at home

FUNCTIONS
1. *Waiter:* 1   3   4   6
   Customer: 2   5   7   8
2. *Possible Answers*
   2. Certainly, ma'am.
   3. I'd like a salad, please.
   4. Can I have a beer, please?
   5. Certainly, sir.
   6. Chocolate.
   7. What flavor would you like?
   8. Yes, sir.
3. *Possible Answers*
   1. Would you like a dessert?
   2. Can I have some french fries?
   3. What flavor would you like?
   4. Can I help you?
   5. Can you bring me the wine
   list?
   6. Do you like the salad?

Lesson 6

GRAMMAR
1. yourself   himself   herself
   itself   ourselves   yourselves
   themselves
2. 1. myself   2. themselves
   3. himself   4. yourself
   5. ourselves
3. *Possible Answers*
   1. They enjoyed themselves at
   the party.   2. She is teaching
   herself to speak French.   3. He
   talks to himself.

VOCABULARY
1. newspaper   toothpaste
   sunglasses   handbag
   raincoat   hamburger
3. a bottle of shampoo   a package
   of cookies   a box of matches
   a tube of toothpaste   a bar of
   chocolate   a can of soup

READING AND FUNCTIONS
1. in a store
2. and 3.   1. False (He wants to
   buy a winter coat.)   2. True
   3. True   4. False (It's too big.)
   5. True   6. True
   7. False (He doesn't buy it
   because it's expensive.)
4. 1. I'll take it.   2. think I'll keep
   looking.

Lesson 7

VOCABULARY
1. *binoculars:* metal, plastic, and
   glass
   wallet: leather or plastic
   umbrella: nylon and metal
   book: paper
2. *Across:* 1. binoculars
   3. umbrella   8. wood   10. hers
   11. metal
   Down: 1. bag   2. camera
   4. round   5. long   6. address
   7. new   9. out

GRAMMAR
1. *Possible Answers*
   1. What shape is it?
   2. What color is it?
   3. What's it made of?
   4. Is this yours?
   5. Whose books are they?
   6. What's in your bag?
2. yours   his   hers   ours   yours
   theirs
3. 2. It's his.   3. It's theirs.
   4. They're ours.   5. They're hers.
   6. It's yours.
4. 2. Whose car is this?
   3. Whose house is this?
   4. Whose binoculars are these?
   5. Whose suitcases are these?
   6. Whose purse is this?

READING AND WRITING
1. 3
2. A: stamps, purse   B: umbrellas
   C: papers, keys, phone card, cash
   card, purse, car keys
   D: nothing
   D is the most careful.

Lesson 8

VOCABULARY

2. 1. c 2. d 3. e 4. a 5. b
3. 1. right 2. problem 3. feel
   4. back 5. throat 6. too bad
4. *Possible Answers*
   1. I have a sore throat.
   2. My back hurts.
   3. I feel faint.
   4. I feel dizzy.
   5. I have a cough.

GRAMMAR AND FUNCTIONS

3. 1. d 2. a 3. c 4. b

READING AND WRITING

1. A sun B insects
3. You shouldn't stay in the sun too long
   You should stay out of the sun around noon
   You should use a sunscreen
   You should lie down in a cool place
   You should call a doctor
   You should take medicine every day

Lesson 9

VOCABULARY

1. *Across:* long good light dry
   big high slow hot fast
   easy small modern
   Down: heavy bad low wet
   old dirty safe dark young
   cold
2. good – better – best
   bad – worse – worst
   heavy – heavier – heaviest
   old – older – oldest
   low – lower – lowest
   easy – easier – easiest
   big – bigger – biggest
   wet – wetter – wettest
3. 1. c 2. e 3. d 4. f 5. b 6. a
4. 2. inches 3. foot/feet
   4. miles per hour 5. miles
   6. square miles
5. 1. feet (ft.) 2. inches (in.)
   3. square miles (sq. mi.)
   4. miles per hour (m.p.h.)
   5. miles (mi.)

READING AND GRAMMAR

1. 1. C 2. A 3. E 4. D 5. B
2. the world's fourth largest country
   The world's second longest river
   the world's widest river
   it covers the largest area
   the country with the highest population
   the 6th highest in the world
   South America's biggest city
   Rio de Janeiro is smaller than São Paulo
   more densely populated
   The warmest months
3. *Possible Answers*
   1. Brazil is smaller than Canada.
   2. Brazil has a bigger population than Chile.
   3. The Nile is narrower than the Amazon.
   4. Rio is smaller than São Paulo.
   5. Most Brazilians live in the cities or on the coast.
4. *Possible Answers*
   1. Brazil is bigger than Argentina.
   2. The Amazon is wider than the Nile.
   3. Brazil has a bigger population than Peru.
   4. Rio is smaller than São Paulo.
   5. June is colder than December.
5. 1. Rio is not as big as São Paulo.
   2. São Paulo is not as warm as Rio.
   3. The climate in the Amazon basin is not as dry as the climate on the coast.
   4. The Amazon is not as long as the Nile.
   5. It is not as warm in June as it is in December.

Lesson 10

VOCABULARY

1. hang gliding   auto racing
   windsurfing   horseback riding
   basketball

GRAMMAR

1. 1. most 2. more 3. most 4. most
   5. more 6. more

READING AND WRITING

1. 2.
2. more polite   more beautiful
   more civilized   better looking
   more sophisticated
   more mouthwatering
   more exotic   more exciting
   more interesting
   more expressive
   more monumental
   more spectacular
3. *Possible Answers*
   Shops are more exciting.
   The ringing of telephones is stranger.
   Bread is tastier.
   Store clerks are more efficient.
   Bank tellers are friendlier.
   Children are politer.
   Street signs are stranger.

Lesson 31

GRAMMAR

2. 1. h 2. d 3. f 4. g 5. b 6. c 7. a
   8. e
3. 1. shouldn't 2. shouldn't
   3. have to 4. can't 5. can't
   6. have to 7. should 8. can't
4. rules and strong advice

READING

1. A 1 B 4
2. *Possible Answers*
   B: keep your dog on a leash
   C: no golf.
   D: no cycling.
   E: no littering
   F: You can't sleep overnight on the benches.
3. You have to wear swimsuits. An adult has to stay with children under six at all times.
4. *Possible Answers*
   Notice A
   You can't litter.
   You can't play golf.
   You can't cycle.
   You have to keep your dog on a leash.
   You can't sleep overnight on the benches.
   You can't stay inside after closing time.
   You can't walk on the flower beds.
   You can't climb the trees.
   Notice B
   You can't wear shorts.
   You can't run or jump.
   You can't smoke in the pool area.
   You can't eat or drink near the pool.

Lesson 12

READING

1. a waitress, an actress, a nanny, a ticket seller, a cook, a zoo-keeper, in telesales
2. Jane Brooks has had fifty-four jobs.   still hasn't found her ideal career.   She has been a model ...I just haven't found...
3. The shortest job she had was as a cook in a cafeteria.   She left after just two hours.
   The longest job she had was as a zoo-keeper.   She stayed at that job for two months.

GRAMMAR

1. *Past participle:* been drunk had driven read left flown taken bought made written sold fought met found eaten gone seen worn
   Past simple: ate had read left saw wore bought made went sold fought met found took flew drove wrote
2. 1. Have you ever been to a foreign country?
   2. He has never appeared on television.
   3. I have visited a lot of countries.
   4. They went to Guatemala last year.
   5. When did they go to Japan?
3. 1. drunk 2. driven
   3. met/ seen 4. worn/bought
   5. flown/ been 6. eaten/had
   7. written/read 8. taken
4. 1. have never been 2. went
   3. has found 4. met
   5. has never flown 6. drank
5. 1. been, went 2. gone, gone, went

Lesson 13

VOCABULARY

Across: 1. neighborhood 4. war
   6. me 7. cash 8. golden
   9. subway 11. since 13. ask
   14. anniversary
Down: 1. New York 2. home
   3. deli 5. retire 7. celebrate
   10. Italy 12. can

GRAMMAR

1. stolen fallen left come
   kept broken run caught
   hurt paid lost found
2. 1. have not caught 2. has fallen
   3. have not found 4. Have you ever broken 5. have kept
3. a ✔ have never visited
   b ✗ visited c ✔ have worked
   d ✗ did you go
   e ✗ visited, had
4. 1. went 2. has ever visited
   3. did you come back
   4. have you lived 5. flew, took
   6. have been married

READING

1. 1. c 2. a 3. d 4. b
2. 1. Jeff and Bill left college ten years ago.
   2. Jeff has been in New York for six months.
   3. Bill has lived in New York since 1993.
   4. Bill has worked for IC since last year.
   5. Jeff has been married for eight years.
   6. Bill has been married for a year.

Lesson 4

VOCABULARY

1. *Across:* 2. matches 4 knife
   6. ice 7. trash 9. glass
   Down: 1. blanket 3. rain
   5. fat 8. has
2. 1. Watch out! 2. Slow down!
   3. Please sit down.
   4. Excuse me. 5. Don't worry!
   6. Be quiet!

GRAMMAR

1. 1. c 2. e 3. a 4. f 5. d 6. b

READING AND WRITING

1. no
3. 1. E 2. B 3. D 4. A 5. C

Lesson 5

VOCABULARY AND GRAMMAR

1. good – bad   quiet – noisy
   careful – careless   polite – rude
   fast – slow   early – late
2. good – well   bad – badly
   happy – happily   fast – fast
   easy – easily   early – early
   angry – angrily   late – late
   careless – carelessly
   fluent – fluently   clear – clearly
   patient – patiently
3. 1. fluently 2. good, bad
   3. patiently/clearly 4. happy
   5. easy, clearly 6. late/early
4. *Possible Answers*
   2. sing: well, badly, loudly
   3. drive: fast, carelessly, well
   4. cook: well
   5. swim: fast
   6. speak English: fluently, badly
   7. laugh: loudly, politely
6. *Possible Answers*
   good well/quickly/carefully
   well good/clear bad/careless

well/fluently   clear/bad
well/hard   easily
7. 1. b   2. d   3. a   4. c
Correct order: 2. d   3. a   1. b   4. c

READING
1. New York
2. slowly   purposefully   slowly
carefully   noisily
3. *Possible Answers*
They walk slowly and
purposefully.
They sit for hours in cafés..
They don't argue about
unimportant things.
They arrive at church early.
They don't have meetings
They don't talk on car phones.
They drive slowly.
They park carefully.
4. *Possible Answers*
They argue about unimportant
things.   They have meetings.
They are noisy.   They shout
They hurry
Taxis honk their horns.

Lesson 16
VOCABULARY AND READING
1. passport control   first class
check in   departure lounge
gas station   baggage reclaim
travel agency   arrival hall
boarding pass
2. c h e i f a g d b
3. *Train*: 2 3 8   *Plane*: 1 4
Car: 5 7 9   *Boat*: 6 10
4. *Positive*: 3   6   8
Negative: 1   2   4   10

GRAMMAR
1. 1. When will he go sightseeing?
2. Will you have a single room?
3. How long will you stay in
Phoenix?
4. How will you get from the
airport/hotel to the hotel/airport?
5. Where will you have dinner
this evening.
2. 1. d   2. e   3. a   4. b   5. c
3. 1. won't   2. 'll   3. won't
4. won't   5. 'll, 'll
5. 1. there won't   2. you will
3. there will   4. we won't
5. they won't

WRITING
1. *Possible Answers*
1. I'll pay cash, then.
2. No, round-trip.
3. I'll have a double room, then.
4. I'll have a steak, then.

Lesson 7
VOCABULARY
1. sunny   cloudy   rainy   foggy
cold   hot   windy   warm
snowy   wet
2. 1. D   2. C   3. F   4. A
5. B   6. E
3. *Possible Answers*
a picnic: sunshine, warm, not too
hot
sailing: sunny and windy, warm

waterskiing: sunny and hot
growing tomatoes: rain, sun, and
warm
skiing: snowy and sunny

GRAMMAR
THIS WILL DEPEND ON FINAL
A/W
1. 1. There will be sunshine. It will
be cold and very windy.
2. It will be sunny and warm. It
will be a nice day.
3. There will be snow. It will be
very cold.
4. It will be rainy and warm.
2. *Possible Answers*
1. It won't rain. It won't be hot.
2. It won't be cold.
3. There won't be any sunshine.
It won't be a nice day.
4. It won't be sunny but it won't be
cold.
4. *Possible Answers*
1. will get   2. will disappear
3. will become   4. will go, will
not grow   5. will have
6. will become

READING
1. *Possible Answers*
Pessimistic: 1   3   6   7   8.   10
Optimistic: 2   4   5   9
2. 1. The book reviewer/critic.
2. Mr. John Bills.
3. *Life Tomorrow*.
4. The problems facing the world
today, possible solutions, and
predictions for the future.
5. Pessimistic for the next fifty
years; optimistic for the more
distant future.

Lesson 38
VOCABULARY AND GRAMMAR
1. invent: dynamite, telephone
grow: rice, oranges, potaoes,
coffee, cotton
discover: Halley's comet,
radioactivity, Jupiter, penicillin
build: house, mosque, church,
the Pyramids
2. 1. grow   2. built   3. discovered
4. grow   5. discovered
6. invented
3. *Present*: 1, 4   *Past*: 2, 3, 5, 6
4. 2. No, it wasn't. It was invented
by Bell.
3. No, it wasn't. It was painted by
Picasso.
4. No, it wasn't. It was written by
Shakespeare.
5. No, they aren't. They are made
in Japan.
6. No, it wasn't. It was built by
Shah Jahan.
5. 2. The pyramids in Egypt were
built by the Pharoahs.
3. Penicillin was discovered by
Fleming in 1928.
4. Oranges are grown Florida.
5. Radioactivity was discovered
by Marie Curie.
6. Gunpowder was invented by
the Chinese in the 9th century.

READING AND WRITING
1. drunk   introduced   appreciated
grown   sold   dried   enjoyed
consumed   heated
2. is grown   are dried and heated
was first grown   was introduced
is grown   is sold
3. 1. China in the 8th century.
2. In the 17th century.
3. India, China, and Sri Lanka.
4. B: coffee   C: tobacco

Lesson 9
VOCABULARY
1. 1. single/round-trip   2.. serving
3.. refreshments   4.. complaint
5.. charge   6.. sightseeing/
camping

GRAMMAR
1. 1. "It's open all year."
2. "It starts at nine thirty."
3. "Dinner is served at seven."
4. "We're late because of the
traffic."
5. "I don't like the food."
6. "I'm not staying another night."
2. 1. was   2. leaves   3. cost   4
were   5. was   6. is   7. was
8. finished
3. 1. He said it wasn't far from
downtown.
2. She said she didn't like opera.
3. She said the bus arrived at
9 o'clock.
4. The manager said that they
had a double room.
5. He said it cost thirty dollars a
day.
6. She said the train took half an
hour.
7. They said they didn't want a
TV in the room.
8. He said they were early and
that it didn't leave until six thirty.
4. 1. left, leaves   2. were, are   3.
cost, costs   4. charged, charges
5. were arriving, are arriving

LISTENING AND WRITING
2. 1. Maria   2. Marjorie   3. Liz
4. Liz
3.   …I have a dentist's
appointment at 1:30 tomorrow so
I can't meet her for lunch but I'll
meet her for coffee at 11 at
Tony's. Can you tell her that if
she doesn't call me back, I will
see here there tomorrow at 11.
Can you also tell her that I got
the books she needed for
college, and they only cost $5
each. Thanks.

Lesson 20
GRAMMAR AND READING
1. 1. went: past simple
2. 'm staying: present continuous
3. 'll come: future simple
4. haven't met: present perfect
5. like: present simple
2. 1. b   2. e   3. a   4. c   5. d
3. *Past simple*: won   spoke

bought   said   stepped   went
came   sent   told   drank
made   arrived   left   lost   took
read   saw   flew   climbed
hurt   found   sold
Present perfect: won   bought
said   stepped   sent   told
eaten   gotten   made   arrived
left   lost   stolen   been   read
written   climbed   gone   hurt
found   sold
4. 1. met   2. came back (last night)
3. have never seen   4. won
5. Have you read   6. arrived
7. received   8. did they leave
5. 1. am staying   2. takes
3. don't like   4. is not playing
5. work   6. Do you often go
6. 1 3 6

READING
1. 1. Michiko.   2. Aya.   3. She is
in Sacramento in California.
4. She is on an English course.
2. 1. d   2. b   3. c   4. a
3. *Possible Answers*
Present simple: As you know, we
work, there are, we speak, we
go, the course finishes, I don't
know
Present continuous: I'm enjoying,
I'm staying
Present perfect: I haven't written,
I have been busy, I've met,
I've seen
Past simple: I left home,
I traveled, the bus ride wasn't
fun, it was, I got sick, we went
sightseeing, I saw
Future: I won't travel, what I'll
do, I'll stay, It'll be, my English
will be